MW00427347

THE MOST DANGEROUS PRESIDENT IN HISTORY

Also by Nick Adams

Retaking America: Crushing Political Correctness
Green Card Warrior: My Quest for Legal Immigration in an Illegals' System
The Case Against the Establishment
Class Dismissed: Why College Isn't the Answer
Trump and Churchill: Defenders of Western Civilization
Trump and Reagan: Defenders of America

THE MOST DANGEROUS PRESIDENT IN HISTORY

NICK ADAMS

A POST HILL PRESS BOOK
ISBN: 978-1-63758-657-0
ISBN (eBook): 978-1-63758-658-7

The Most Dangerous President in History

Cover design by Cody Corcoran

Post Hill Press
New York • Nashville
posthillpress.com

Published in the United States of America
1 2 3 4 5 6 7 8 9 10

TABLE OF CONTENTS

INTRODUCTION

President Joe Biden is the most dangerous president and one of the worst presidents, if not *the* worst president, America has ever seen. Throughout this book, I will prove to you why President Biden is the most dangerous president. Numerous examples to share with your friends and family will be provided.

He is not necessarily an evil man, but the policies he supports and the way he approaches politics are dangerous for America and put us on unsolid ground. His social policies are those of grown men in women's bathrooms, abortion through all nine months of pregnancy paid for by taxpayers, and letting critical race theorists and diversity officer-types—instead of strategists and warriors—run our military. He does not believe in a policy of putting America first. His policies look more like those of a left-wing organizing meeting than those of Main Street America.

America deserves a president who will put the country first. Leftists, RINOs, and the mainstream media will try to tell you that American nationalism is about race—but it's not. America First and American nationalism means putting our country—black, white, Hispanic, Jewish, Catholic, poor, rich—before the goals of NATO, the United Nations, and the International Monetary Fund. It means that our foreign policy should primarily be aimed at boosting America's economy and protecting our borders from foreign threats. It does not mean sending our brave men and women in uniform to dozens of countries to protect *those countries' borders* from invasion or attack.

It means that we think of the Kentucky farmer, the New York City restaurant owner, and the manufacturing CEO in Texas before we think about what the elites at Davos or the United Nations want us to do. We deserve a president who wakes up every morning thinking about how we can boost economic activity and help the family in Montana, Virginia, or Maine, not how we can help increase the profits of international bankers. We think about how to keep our citizens safe and employed, and *then* we can have a discussion about how many immigrants and refugees we decide to have come here.

That's what President Donald Trump did. He thought every day about how to help the laid-off factory worker in Ohio or the lobster fisherman in Maine—not necessarily about what Klaus Schwab or Bill Gates wanted. Black employment soared. Hispanic employment soared. The price of gas and all fuel sources remained low, helping everyone prosper as American manufacturing saw a comeback under the nationalist economic policy of Trump and Peter Navarro.

But that changed in January 2021, when a globalist, leftist president took office and decided to pursue policies that would harm patriotic Americans who just want to go to church, provide for their families, and have a chance to enjoy life without worrying if gas is going to go up to eight dollars a gallon, if groceries for a family of four are going to go up to $600 a week, and if China is going to continue to pillage our economy.

President Joe Biden has come into office and surrounded himself with America Last, Goldman Sachs-McKinsey consultants who seek to appease the United Nations and the *New York Times* before appeasing the family in Ohio, the small business owner in Texas, or the entrepreneur in North Dakota. He wants to ensure that abortion giant Planned Parenthood continues to receive half a billion dollars a year in taxpayer money so it can butcher babies. He wants to ensure that the Green movement, which seeks to end all use of fossil fuels and whose economic policies will drive us into literal darkness, is appeased. He wants to make sure that MSNBC and the *New York Times* editorial board say nice things about him. In other words, he is not focused on people like you and me.

His economic policy is definitively not America First. It is the economic policy of Alexandria Ocasio-Cortez (AOC), Bernie Sanders, and Elizabeth Warren, which ultimately is the economic policy of Karl Marx. It is about asking the United Nations and other countries to help us reduce our carbon emissions while China laughs all the way to the bank and continues to rip us off using intellectual property theft and currency manipulation. It's about letting Russia build a pipeline—while putting thousands of hard-working union guys out of work and making you pay more at the pump so the Sierra Club or the other envirowackos will give Biden a nice award for saving the planet. I personally think that our economic policy should be driven with the average guy in mind, not what Al Gore or John Kerry thinks is a good idea.

His foreign policy mixes with his social policies to create boondoggles and deadly results, as brave troops were left to die in Afghanistan while Biden's generals were studying white privilege and the works of leftist racial radical Ibram X. Kendi. Our military were left to die while General Lloyd Austin read about how to be an "antiracist." It is truly despicable how President Biden has governed. He has also failed to lead on Ukraine, taking action and inaction that has led to thousands of dead Ukrainians as of this writing. His anti-American energy policies have enriched Vladimir Putin while leaving you and me poorer.

He has appointed far-left radicals who want to see the destruction of the American economy and American energy independence. He appointed not a medical or public health professional or scientist to run the Department of Health and Human Services (HHS) but a staunch advocate for abortion. Xavier Becerra is an attorney who used his power as California Attorney General (AG) to target innocent Catholic nuns who provide charitable care to poor, elderly people. This is not someone whose background is in expanding access to affordable medication or who has experience in developing new treatments for cancer, diabetes, or high blood pressure. This is an ideologue who is committed to abortion, even if it means using the power of the state to hunt down pro-life journalists who expose wrongdoing by Planned Parenthood and the abortion industry.

Biden has appointed an Energy Secretary who sang about ending gasoline use, oversaw a terrible economy in Michigan, and repeatedly gave taxpayer dollars to so-called green energy companies that failed to create the jobs promised. Jennifer Granholm does not wake up every day and think about how to ensure clean natural gas and oil flow through safe pipelines so we can fill up our cars, heat our homes, and power the American economy.

Biden wants a far-left judge, Ketanji Brown Jackson, to sit on the Supreme Court for decades and pursue a leftist agenda. He has allowed his economic policy not to be driven by the interests of Middle America but instead by the AOC-Bernie Sanders Green New Deal wing of the Democratic Party.

What also makes Biden dangerous is the way the media and his handlers still try to sell the American voters a different President Biden; he's the guy you'd sit down at the bar and have a beer with. You'd see him marching on the picket lines to demand higher wages with his union pals. Biden dining at the fanciest restaurants? No, c'mon man! He eats a burger with a Coke just like you and me.

Not.

Many voters, particularly those in the "Boomer" generation, may still have a view of Biden as the lovable, working-class guy who makes some gaffes from time to time, but that's just part of his charm, right? Sure, he orchestrated a factless assault on Clarence Thomas, one of this country's most brilliant minds, but that's just politics, c'mon man!

In reality, President Biden has continually undermined America's image in the world, wrecked a booming economy, and continued to divide the country through his hapless "leadership" on coronavirus. He has opened up the borders to anyone who wants to enter here, sign up for welfare, and stay forever, never having to go through the legal process to become an American citizen.

Biden has used the coronavirus vaccines to divide America, urging companies to fire people who have made the personal decision not to take it. He has blamed the pandemic on them and urged ostracizing them. Hard-working nurses who put themselves on the front line to help heal and provide comfort to our elderly and medically vulnerable were fired from their jobs at the urging of Biden's pro-vaccine mandate policies.

Rhetoric against people who have made different decisions about vaccines than he has is reaching dangerous levels, and cities even implemented passport systems meant to shame free American citizens for not getting a vaccine. President Biden quickly sued states such as Georgia, which implemented basic voter integrity laws, but has not done anything to stop his leftist allies in Chicago and Philly and Boston from requiring free American citizens to show their medical records in order to eat inside a restaurant or watch a movie. What's next? Will we have to bring copies of our latest physicals to buy a car?

Biden is the most dangerous president, and throughout this book I will provide you with numerous examples of why he is dangerous and why he must be out of office in 2024.

CHAPTER 1

BIDEN SHUTS DOWN THE ECONOMY, NOT THE VIRUS

"I'm not going to shut down the economy. I'm not going to shut down the country, but I am going to shut down the virus."

*-**President Biden,** October 2020*[1]

Despite Biden's claims in the waning days of the 2020 election that he was "not going to shut down the economy" but he was going to "shut down the virus," the hapless and dangerous leader *did* shut down the economy but *did not* shut down the virus.

1 "Biden promises to 'shut down the virus' if elected," Yahoo!, October 2020, https://news.yahoo.com/biden-promises-shut-down-virus-190000061.html

Within days of taking office, the Biden-Harris White House falsely claimed that Donald Trump's administration had not left any sort of plans for the rollout of the COVID-19 vaccine, developed under Operation Warp Speed. The claim revolves around an anonymous source and primarily one story on CNN.[2]

With that story, and the administration's promotion of it, Biden decided that he would start his term in office by maligning Trump and dividing Americans. He refused to let go of Trump and instead had to begin, on day one, with blaming his predecessor. This claim is, of course, obviously false on its face. Are we to believe that none of the thousands of employees of the Departments of Health and Human Services, Defense, or Labor were working on distribution plans for the vaccines? Are we to believe that the billions of dollars spent on coronavirus aid did not include any more for a rollout of the vaccine? Are we to believe that Pfizer, Johnson & Johnson, and other vaccine manufacturers produced the COVID shots without any forethought on how they'd get into people's arms? Of course not, but left-wing CNN and a few anonymous sources inside the White House needed something to pin on Trump and, with that story, set the tone that the Biden administration would not be one that took responsibility and ownership.

---

2 MJ Lee, "Biden inheriting nonexistent coronavirus vaccine distribution plan and must 'start from scratch' sources say," CNN, January 21, 2021, https://www.cnn.com/2021/01/21/politics/biden-covid-vaccination-trump/index.html

Even public health emperor Dr. Anthony Fauci dismissed the claim, going on the record with his comments, unlike CNN's anonymous sources. "We're certainly not starting from scratch, because there is activity going on in the distribution," Fauci said. Just days prior to the fake news CNN article, over thirteen million Americans had already gotten the shots.[3]

In fact, the whole of Biden's COVID-19 policy appeared to be thrown together at different times, lacked direction, and further divided hard-working Americans. We know, of course, that on the campaign Biden said that everyone would just need to mask up for one hundred days and the virus would end. He then appointed an attorney, Xavier Becerra, to lead HHS. Becerra's primary "health" experience, as we will discuss later, is stopping the merger of hospitals because they would not commit so-called "sex change operations." He also helped take Catholic nuns to court for not covering abortifacient birth control.

Biden said he would not mandate vaccines. Then that changed, and Biden flip-flopped again, pursuing a number of vaccine mandates on hard-working Americans while encouraging businesses to pursue them too. Frontline workers of 2020 who treated COVID patients became 2021's "unvaccinated" individuals who made the personal decision not to take the COVID shots. Biden continued

---

3 Leandra Bernstein, "How Biden's vaccine distribution strategy is different from Trump's," NBC, January 19, 2021, https://nbcmontana.com/news/nation-world/how-bidens-vaccine-distribution-strategy-is-different-from-trumps

to divide the country, pushing the lie that there was a "pandemic of the unvaccinated."[4]

But, if Americans had not been hammered enough by on-again, off-again COVID shutdowns, bare shelves, and seeing events canceled, the Biden-Harris White House had more plans up their sleeves, including putting into place job-killing executive orders from the very beginning that later would lead to record inflation.

Biden shuts down at least 25 percent of natural gas and oil

The U.S. economy was recovering and returning to the record levels of employment and wealth under the Trump presidency. As with the vaccine, President Biden was given a great situation, as people were primed to spend money after being cooped up inside and many events and businesses began to reopen.[5] Many Americans were already fed up with the COVID shutdowns and had been saving money and were ready to get back to work and leisure.

Yet, the Biden-Harris White House, instead of thinking about the concerns of Main Street, decided to hand

---

4 Aditi Sangal, Adrienne Vogt, Melissa Mahtani and Meg Wagner, "Covid-19 vaccine booster doses approved for some US adults," CNN, https://edition.cnn.com/us/live-news/coronavirus-pandemic-vaccine-updates-09-24-21/h_0f8fab1a204b-09d660a23aa3c1e32954

5 Alex Gailey, "How Has the Pandemic Impacted U.S. Savings Rates," *TIME*, August 30, 2021, https://time.com/nextadvisor/banking/savings/us-saving-rate-soaring/

over its environmental and economic agenda to AOC and Bernie Sanders.

Biden and Harris decided to effectively let Russia and the Saudis dominate the energy market while slamming hard-working Americans with higher oil and gas prices.

Promising to "listen to science" to face the "profound climate crisis," Biden took several executive actions that effectively limited at least 25 percent of oil and gas exploration.[6]

"To the extent consistent with applicable law, the Secretary of the Interior shall pause new oil and natural gas leases on public lands or in offshore waters pending completion of a comprehensive review and reconsideration of Federal oil and gas permitting and leasing practices in light of the Secretary of the Interior's broad stewardship responsibilities over the public lands and in offshore waters, including potential climate and other impacts associated with oil and gas activities on public lands or in offshore waters," one executive order said.

This has and had major implications, according to a national security organization that analyzed the executive actions. Put simply, it was the Green New Deal in action: pausing new oil and gas production.

---

6 "Executive Order on Tackling the Climate Crisis at Home and Abroad," The White House, January 27, 2021, https://www.whitehouse.gov/briefing-room/presidential-actions/2021/01/27/executive-order-on-tackling-the-climate-crisis-at-home-and-abroad/

"Federal land accounts for about 24 percent of oil and gas production in the United States, mainly in the offshore Gulf of Mexico," the Center for Strategic and International Studies (CSIS) explained.[7] While CSIS tried to run cover for Biden and downplay the short-term effects, we've all seen gas prices skyrocket enough to know that they were too optimistic or too naive.

"U.S. GDP could decline by a cumulative $700 billion by 2030," the American Petroleum Institute warned. "U.S. households could spend a cumulative $19 billion more on energy by 2030."[8]

The situation reached an embarrassing moment for the Democratic Party when leaders from New Mexico begged Biden to exempt them from the restrictions, as the southwestern state derives a significant amount of tax revenue and economic activity from oil and gas. Of course, like most limousine liberals, New Mexico Democrats wanted *everyone else* to be restricted, just not in their state, where constituents could vote them out if they lost their jobs or had to pay five dollars per gallon at the pump.

"New Mexico's Democratic Governor is pushing for her state to get a waiver from the Biden administration's

---

7 Ben Cahill, "Biden Makes Sweeping Changes to Oil and Gas Policy," Center for Strategic & International Studies, January 28, 2021, https://www.csis.org/analysis/biden-makes-sweeping-changes-oil-and-gas-policy

8 "A Federal Leasing and Development Ban Threatens America's Energy Security and Economic Growth, Undermines Environmental Progress," American Petroleum Institute, https://www.api.org/news-policy-and-issues/exploration-and-production/federal-leasing-and-development-ban-study

pause on new oil and gas leasing on federal lands," Reuters reported in March 2021.[9]

The state's two Democratic senators also begged Biden to spare their state from the devastating crackdown.

"In recent letters to the Biden administration, New Mexico Democrat U.S. Sens. Martin Heinrich and Ben Ray Lujan called on the Biden administration to provide federal relief to New Mexico as slowing oil and gas production could negatively impact the state's economy," the *Carlsbad Current Argus* reported in March 2021.

"As the department considers longer term policies to reduce greenhouse gas pollution and limit climate change, we ask for your assistance in ensuring that states like New Mexico receive assistance in making the transition to a zero carbon economy," the letter said.

"Oil and gas workers and communities they live in have helped build our nation for more than a century, and revenues from mineral production have supported New Mexico's educational system and state budget," the senators said.[10]

In addition to being bad for the economy, this sort of policymaking is, of course, bad for America. It sends the message that oil workers in Texas or Oklahoma can lose

---

9 "New Mexico seeking exemption from Biden oil and gas leasing pause–governor," Reuters, March 11, 2021, https://www.reuters.com/article/us-usa-drilling-new-mexico-idUKKBN2B333V

10 Adrian Hedden, "Biden's review of oil and gas leasing moves forward amid concern from New Mexico leaders," Current Argus, March 12, 2021, https://www.currentargus.com/story/news/local/2021/03/12/new-mexico-concerned-biden-admin-advances-oil-and-gas-leasing-review/6922116002/

their jobs but New Mexicans should be protected because their senators share the party with the president.

However, even as gas prices soar to this day, President Biden continues to pursue the goals of the Green New Deal, to continually end the use of oil and gas. The plan is, of course, to make it so expensive that people will have to switch to expensive solar and other "renewable" forms of energy.

"The Federal Energy Regulatory Commission moved… to more rigorously consider the effects of climate change in weighing whether to approve proposed gas pipelines or related infrastructure projects," the *Washington Examiner* reported February 17, 2022. "The decision will make it more difficult to build infrastructure for fossil fuels, an outcome sought by environmentalists."[11] This will, of course, make fossil fuels more expensive, but—for bike-riding or train-riding leftists who live in NYC or D.C.—it doesn't matter to them. Meanwhile, you and your small business with five or six trucks and your crews have to pay sixty dollars or seventy dollars at a time to fill up. The people who keep this country running, not the high-paid bureaucrats in D.C., aren't going to buy the new electric vehicles (EVs), with or without a tax credit.

But that's what Biden and AOC and the rest of their party want. Consider this. "House Democrats are pushing for the passage of a $2,500 federal credit for used electric

---

11 Jeremy Beaman, "FERC sets new environmental hurdles for gas pipeline approvals," *Washington Examiner*, February 17, 2022, https://www.washingtonexaminer.com/policy/ferc-sets-new-environmental-hurdles-for-gas-pipeline-approvals

vehicle purchases as well as a $7,500 credit for new EVs and an extra $4,500 for union-made EVs," *Just the News* reported on February 19, 2022.[12]

This is one of those policies that seems innocuous: get a tax credit for buying an EV! But, in reality, it is an out-of-touch policy. First, there are only a handful of companies that qualify for the higher tax credit. Encouraging American manufacturing is a good thing, but there is no reason to pit union workers against nonunion workers. Republicans have also pointed out that this was a divisive proposal when it was first proposed under the Build Back Better legislation. "Eleven governors complained that the more generous tax credit for cars made in union plants would punish companies and workers in their states," the Associated Press reported in November 2021. "Republican lawmakers portray it as payback for a major Democratic benefactor, the United Auto Workers, which spent about $1.25 million in support of federal candidates in the 2020 elections, more than 99% for Democratic candidates, according to OpenSecrets, which tracks campaign money."[13]

---

12 Nicholas Ballasy, "Dems push $2,500 tax credit for used EVs, up to $12,500 for new union EVs in rush to '100% use,'" Just the News, February 19, 2022, https://justthenews.com/government/congress/house-democrats-support-passing-2500-federal-credit-used-ev-purchases

13 Kevin Freking, "Biden bill includes boost for union-made electric vehicles," ABC News, November 11, 2021, https://abcnews.go.com/Business/wireStory/biden-bill-includes-boost-union-made-electric-vehicles-81108913

Second, the cost of most EVs is out of the price range of many Americans. There is currently a $7,500 EV credit, but companies like Tesla are excluded under the previous rules because they have sold too many cars. It's not clear if the new policy, if implemented, would remove the cap. Some of the cars are also major fire hazards. For example, when you look up Chrysler's Pacifica Hybrid, the top results are about how it is a fire risk to plug the car in inside. Just keep your garage open for the criminals and run a cord from your house outside. I'm sure that is not a great strategy for Michiganders when it is ten degrees below freezing! "Chrysler is recalling 16,741 Pacifica minivans due to a potential fire risk that could occur even if the vehicle is off. As a result, it recommends that owners park the vehicles outside and away from other vehicles and buildings," Carscoops.com reported on February 15, 2022.[14]

Even CNN raised some red flags about the dangers of electric cars. "At the end of September [2020], BMW initiated a recall in the United States of 10 different BMW and Mini plug-in hybrid models because of a risk of fire caused by debris that may have gotten into battery cells during manufacturing," CNN reported in November 2020. "Then, in early October, the National Highway Traffic Safety Administration opened an investigation

---

14 Sebastien Ball, "Chrysler Pacifica PHEV Owners Shouldn't Charge Their Minivan Or Park It Inside Due To Fire Risk," Carscoops, February 15, 2022, https://www.carscoops.com/2022/02/chrysler-pacifica-phev-owners-shouldnt-charge-their-minivan-or-park-it-inside-due-to-fire-risk/

into reports of apparently spontaneous battery fires in Chevrolet Bolt EVs. GM says it is cooperating with the investigation."[15]

"A few days later, Hyundai announced that it was recalling 6,700 Kona Electric SUVs in the United States, among about 75,000 of that model to be recalled worldwide, after it had received numerous reports of vehicles catching fire while parked," CNN reported. While it noted that "electric car battery fires remain infrequent occurrences," it is worth asking if we should rush to continue to spend money on EVs while many gasoline cars work just fine. This type of tax credit also hurts middle-income Americans because it encourages manufacturers to invest more money in EVs instead of reliable diesel or gasoline cars.

Incredibly, as gas prices continued to surge, President Biden blamed Putin for the hike in prices, which began far before the Russian president invaded Ukraine. Biden failed to take responsibility for his actions and claimed he did not do anything to limit domestic oil production.

"It is simply not true that my administration or policies are holding back domestic energy production," Biden said in March 2022. "That is simply not true."[16]

---

15 Peter Valdes-Dapena, "Electric car batteries are catching fire and that could be a big turnoff to buyers," CNN Business, November 10, 2020, https://www.cnn.com/2020/11/10/success/electric-car-vehicle-battery-fires/index.html

16 Thomas Catenacci, "'Simply Not True': Biden Says He Isn't Holding Back US Energy Production," *Daily Caller*, March 8, 2022, https://dailycaller.com/2022/03/08/joe-biden-white-house-domestic-energy-production-russia/

As we have seen so far, and as described further in this book, he has clearly started a war against American energy independence.

Oil company executives, the people who actually oversee production of American energy, have come out against Biden's assertions.

"The United States has shown its global energy dominance over the past decade. Unfortunately, this has been threatened by the current Administration's policies against domestic natural gas and oil production," Independent Petroleum Association of America COO Jeff Eshelman told *The Daily Caller* in March 2022.

Others agree.

"President Biden, on day one of his presidency, made it his top priority to cripple American oil and gas producers," Cecil O'Brate, CEO of American Warrior Oil, told Fox Business in March 2022.[17] "His administration has axed progress on the Keystone pipeline, shut down leases on federal lands, encouraged Woke Wall Street to divest from fossil fuels, and installed absolute antagonists in leadership at Federal Reserve, the EPA and Department of Interior."

The governor of Alaska also said that this claim is untrue and that Biden is indeed responsible for the shutdown of American energy. Governor Mike Dunleavy noted, for example, that the Biden administration failed

---

17 Marisa Schultz, "Cecil O'Brate, CEO of American Warrior Oil in Kansas blames Biden for high gas prices," Fox Business, March 9, https://www.foxbusiness.com/politics/oil-producer-calls-out-bidens-energy-policies

to defend a ConocoPhillips pipeline in Alaska, in addition to other actions detailed here so far.

Alaska governor puts Biden in his place—gas prices are your fault!

"Mr. President you said your policies are not holding back domestic energy production. This will be a true statement when you reverse course and allow energy projects to get back on the track they were on before you took office," Governor Dunleavy said in a March 10, 2022, news release.

"You can lower the price at the pump for Americans by expediting the permitting and regulating processes on responsible oil and gas projects," he said. "The U.S. should not be begging for oil from dictatorships such as Iran and Venezuela. We can produce it at home with the highest of standards for environmental protection, if you will simply let us."

He gave several examples of how the Biden-AOC-Harris White House has undermined American energy independence.

He wrote:[18]

- Defend the Willow project in the National Petroleum Reserve-Alaska, NPR-A. Your

---

18 Mike Dunleavy, "High Energy Costs Drive up Inflation, Call for Domestic Oil," Office of Governor Mike Dunleavy (The Great State of Alaska), March 10, 2022, https://gov.alaska.gov/newsroom/2022/03/10/high-energy-costs-drive-up-inflation-call-for-domestic-oil/

administration did not appeal a federal court judgment that reversed an approval. Defend the project in the supplemental EIS [Environmental Impact Statement]. With a resource estimate of 450 million to 800 million barrels of oil equivalent, Willow is the largest standalone oil development on the North Slope in more than 20 years. It is nearly shovel ready, could be built by 2025-2026, and would supply some 160,000 barrels of oil per day.

- Restore the leases your administration suspended on oil and gas in ANWR, the Arctic National Wildlife Refuge.
- Undo the recently reverted management plan of the NPR-A, which prohibits development on 6.7 million acres. Between the development of NPR-A and the 1002 Area of ANWR, Alaska could place an additional ~17 billion barrels of oil and an additional 32 Tcf [trillion cubic feet] of gas in the marketplace.
- The Alaska Gasline Project has key permits and federal loan guarantees in place. A Wood Mackenzie report estimates that Alaska's LNG pricing would be lower than that of other U.S. projects competing for the same Asian market. Your Administration can stop issuing anti-fossil fuel statements to encourage investment in

> domestic energy production. Withdraw your motion for remand in February to the Ambler Road project. If allowed to be developed, the project would provide a supply of strategic minerals needed for renewable energy projects, electronics, and military defense.

Will Biden take these steps? Not likely. Following the principle that "personnel is policy," it is clear that the Biden-Harris-AOC administration wants to limit, if not end, oil and gas usages.

Several of Biden's appointees have made it explicitly clear that they want it to be painful for companies to invest in oil and gas technologies and exploration.

Biden nominates anti-oil and anti-gas personnel to financial roles

When a president nominates someone to the DOE or Interior, we're more likely to know to be on the lookout for any views that would indicate that they oppose oil and natural gas.

But what is scarier is how the Biden-Harris-AOC agenda includes putting people in places of power to oversee banking and the financial system who have a stated record of wanting to see oil and gas companies go bankrupt. They will likely use the levers of the financial system to force companies into pursuing their personal hard-left agenda.

Remember that it does not take a specific law to scare companies about the government; all it takes is one letter or one speech from someone in power hinting that it appears that something might be amiss.

Here's what I mean: The Biden-Harris-Sanders team wanted Cornell Professor Saule Omarova appointed Comptroller of the Currency. While, thankfully, Republicans defeated her nomination and forced her to withdraw, her appointment shows how the Biden team thinks. Professor Omarova does not need to find that banks under her supervision violated a specific law; she does not need to go through the formal process of referring civil complaints over to the SEC for prosecution. All it takes is one phone call or one letter from a staffer working for her to the legal counsel of banks that asks questions.

In this way, Biden and his team can use the threats of prosecution to force companies to submit to their far-left ideological agenda.

Who is Professor Omarova and why is it so dangerous that she, or someone like her, could be put in charge of supervising banks?

"The way we basically get rid of those carbon financiers is that we starve them of their sources of capital," Omarova had said some time prior to her nomination. By "carbon financiers" she means banks that loan money to oil and gas companies.

Omarova, who, remember, would have tremendous power to shape financial policy and advocate for changes, said she wanted to end private banking "as we know it."

In October 2020, she proposed "The People's Ledger," a leftist reengineering of our banking system, which would "radically redefine the role of a central bank as the ultimate public platform for generating, modulating, and allocating financial resources in a democratic economy."[19]

"By separating their lending function from their monetary function, the proposed reform will effectively 'end banking,' as we know it," Omarova wrote.[20]

That's what we know she wrote; we have no idea what she wrote as a student at Moscow State University, except that her undergraduate thesis was titled "Karl Marx's Economic Analysis and the Theory of Revolution in The Capital."

"These are very, very radical ideas. In fact, I don't think I've ever seen a more radical choice for any regulatory spot in our federal government," Senator Pat Toomey warned. He tried to obtain Omarova's thesis. "While it appears that you have deleted any reference to your thesis in the version of your curriculum vitae (CV) that is cur-

19 Matt Lamb, "Cornell professor who wanted to 'starve' oil companies withdraws Treasury nomination," The College Fix, December 10, 2021, https://www.thecollegefix.com/cornell-professor-who-wanted-to-starve-oil-companies-withdraws-treasury-nomination/

20 Saule T. Omarova, "The People's Ledger: How to Democratize Money and Finance the Economy," *Cornell Legal Studies Research Paper* no. 20–45. (2020): 1–71. https://papers.ssrn.com/sol3/papers.cfm?abstract_id=3715735

rently available on the Cornell Law School website, the paper appeared on your CV as recently as April 2017," Toomey wrote.[21]

Omarova was defeated, which is great news, but the anti-energy nominees keep coming.

Biden nominated Sarah Bloom Raskin, a professor and the wife of anti-Trump Representative Jamie Raskin, to the Federal Reserve. The Federal Reserve, as you probably know, has immense power. Thankfully, she withdrew after Senator Manchin said he would not vote for her. But let's take a look at her views because it tells us what the priorities are of the Biden-Harris-AOC White House.

She's a radical. At a time while gas prices are skyrocketing, Biden wants to bring someone in who wants to see oil companies die.

"The coronavirus pandemic has laid bare just how vulnerable the United States is to sudden, catastrophic shocks. Climate change poses the next big threat. Ignoring it, particularly to the benefit of fossil fuel interests, is a risk we can't afford," she wrote in May 2020. "From my time as a Federal Reserve governor and then deputy Treasury secretary, I've learned that times like this not only can determine our ability to recover from a crisis but can also help inoculate us against the next one. That's why it is imperative that we make investments now that will

---

21 Hannah Lalgie, "Senator demands Biden nominee's college thesis on Karl Marx's 'economic analysis,'" The College Fix, October 18, 2021, https://www.thecollegefix.com/senator-demands-biden-nominees-college-thesis-on-karl-marxs-economic-analysis/

increase the resilience of our economy," Raskin wrote in the *New York Times.*[22]

"The decision to bring oil and gas into the Fed's investment portfolio not only misdirects limited recovery resources but also sends a false price signal to investors about where capital needs to be allocated," she wrote further.

I agree that the government should not be picking winners and losers. We should have a simple tax and regulatory system that lets all companies fairly and freely compete. People who want to pay more for solar or wind power can freely choose that option; that's the beauty of a free-market economy.

But that's not Raskin's position nor that of the Biden administration's; they do want to pump trillions of dollars into solar and wind and other projects that will produce very little in terms of energy and reliability at least for decades.

When asked by Senator John Kennedy why Raskin made those statements, she struggled to explain.

"The Fed should not pick or favor any sector at all," Raskin, the Federal Reserve nominee, told Kennedy. But, in June 2020, she sang a different tune. She wanted the Federal Reserve to label investments in oil and gas companies as risky. In fact, she has consistently advocated for using government power to strangle energy companies.

---

22 Sarah Bloom Raskin, "Why Is the Fed Spending so much Money on a Dying Industry," *New York Times,* May 28, 2020, https://www.nytimes.com/2020/05/28/opinion/fed-fossil-fuels.html

Professor Larry Bell of the University of Houston provided a few examples in a February 2022 opinion piece for *Newsmax*.[23]

"Despite pledging to abide by objective monetary banking policy interests, fully expect instead that Sarah Ruskin will use the Fed to push Environmental, Social, and Governance (ESG) lending qualification scores which include assessments of impacts on climate change," Bell warned.

"Informed decisions allow us to mitigate the financial impact of climate risks and fashion timely remedies ahead of a crisis," Raskin said in March 2020.[24] Bell points out that this is a call for regulators to "foster the development of climate-related financial risk management technology."

This would include, in Bell's words, "climate-related financial disclosures and stress tests."

"Raskin urged in a June 2020 Ceres article that the Fed use its risk-based standards to drive capital away from oil and natural-gas firms toward 'sustainable investments,' and went so far as to suggest that the Fed should de-bank energy companies by establishing portfolio or concentra-

---

23 Larry Bell, "Biden Fed Pick Will Plug Fossil Fuel Finance Pipeline," *Newsmax*, February 9, 2022, https://www.newsmax.com/larrybell/sarah-raskin-fossil-fuel-federal-reserve/2022/02/09/id/1056124/

24 Sarah Bloom Raskin, "Testimony of the Honorable Sarah Bloom Raskin Before the Senate Democrats' Special Committee on the Climate Crisis," The FinReg Blog, March 17, 2020, https://sites.law.duke.edu/thefinregblog/2020/03/17/testimony-of-the-honorable-sarah-bloom-raskin-before-the-senate-democrats-special-committee-on-the-climate-crisis/

tion limits for banks on 'high-emission assets,'" Professor Bell warned.[25]

It makes her a perfect fit to carry out the Biden-Harris-Bernie Sanders agenda where the government forces and intimidates companies out of drilling for oil and gas.

For example, the Biden administration has pursued climate disclosures that force companies to calculate climate risks from their businesses. This can then be used as leverage, it has been theorized, to dissuade investors from putting money into those companies.

"The Biden administration is prioritizing proposed rulemaking that would require companies to produce climate-related disclosures, most notably through the Securities and Exchange Commission, a form of indirect pressure on fossil fuel companies," the *Washington Examiner* reported in February 2022.[26]

"The SEC is debating the extent to which it can compel companies to disclose details about how much energy they buy and how they handle climate risks," the *Washington Examiner* reported. "Such self-reported disclosures to investors have already become commonplace in business, and adding government-mandated ESG disclosure rules is a big goal for the administration."

---

25 "Addressing Climate as a Systemic Risk: a call to action for U.S. financial regulators," Ceres, https://www.ceres.org/resources/reports/addressing-climate-systemic-risk

26 Zachary Halaschak, "Biden looks to pressure investors away from fossil fuels via climate disclosures," *Washington Examiner*, February 18, 2022, https://www.washingtonexaminer.com/policy/economy/biden-looks-to-pressure-investors-away-from-fossil-fuels-via-climate-disclosures

The plan has the backing of far-left U.S. Senator Elizabeth Warren, a proponent of heavy-handed government control over the economy. She is pushing Biden to go hard and fast to punish companies that do not embrace the Green New Deal Communist agenda.

"I urge you to act quickly and to release the strongest requirements possible to begin the formal rulemaking process," Senator Warren wrote to SEC Chair Gary Gensler in February 2022, according to Reuters.[27] "These delays are unwarranted and unacceptable, and violate the commitment, which you made seven months ago…the absence of a rule leaves shareholders and investors in the dark about the significant long- and short-term climate risks facing public companies."

This is dangerous and divisive. It is taking a regulatory body with a specific mission and using it to push a far-left political agenda. The general mission of the SEC is to ensure that companies are being honest with shareholders—and holding them accountable if a company misleads investors, for example, lying to them about the development of a new drug or a new line of products.

Furthermore, it seems safe to say that Senator Warren wants a *specific* result from the analysis of climate risks. She very likely wants companies to have to tell investors that climate change is going to harm their investments

27 Katanga Johnson, "U.S. Senator Warren 'urges' SEC chief to issue new climate rule after delays," Reuters, February 10, 2022, https://www.reuters.com/markets/commodities/us-senator-warren-urges-sec-chief-issue-new-climate-rule-after-delays-2022-02-10/

and then they'll be more supportive of top-down controls on the economy and oil and gas production.

But each company would have a separate analysis done, and it seems safe to say that, if those corporations reach a different conclusion than Senator Warren's, she'll haul them in front of a Senate committee. She is, after all, the person who used her government office to try to intimidate Amazon to stop selling a book by COVID contrarian Dr. Joseph Mercola and others.[28]

But this is part of the dangerous and divisive Biden agenda: to use government agencies to attack freedom of speech and economic liberty. It does not take a new law; it just takes a strong nudge from a government agency with regulatory authority to push companies to get in line.

Inflation skyrockets in Biden's first two years

President Trump had a booming economy because he combined a number of smart policies that helped the American worker. He pursued policies to make it easier for oil and gas companies to operate, which then lowered the cost of manufacturing and other business expenses. At the same time, he sought to restrict immigration to this country, especially of low-skilled workers, thus creating a tight labor market that helped wages increase.

But the Biden-Harris team decided to drive up inflation through anti-oil and -gas prices while also implement-

---

28 Elizabeth Warren to Andy Jassy, September 7, 2021, https://www.warren.senate.gov/imo/media/doc/2021.9.7%20Letter%20to%20Amazon%20on%20COVID%20Misinformation.pdf

ing other dumb policies like vaccine mandates, which made it harder to find qualified workers, and pumping trillions of dollars into the economy.

Inflation hits people the hardest the poorer they are. Biden's inflation is due to the Democrats' pumping trillions of dollars into the economy, shutting down oil and gas, and supporting the firing of thousands and thousands of workers through unethical vaccine mandates.

Of course, the Biden administration began its time in office by claiming that the inflation would just be "transitory." Everyone who had taken at least two economics courses could tell that this was completely false.

Treasury Secretary Janet Yellen, who previously pushed disastrous policies while at the Federal Reserve, ran interference for Biden and said that inflation would just be "transitory" along with Biden's other economic advisers.

Yellen, who is supposed to be a financial wizard, either lied to the American people or lacks the ability to understand how increased spending, regulatory restrictions, and inflation work—a scary notion if she's a professor, but a dangerous one if she's the Treasury Secretary.

The mainstream media rushed to trumpet her views, as leftist media types love Janet Yellen. The trillions pumped into the economy and the high energy prices were just "transitory" Biden's economic team said. "I don't believe that inflation will be an issue but if it becomes an issue, we have tools to address it. These are historic investments that we need to make our economy productive and fair," she said about increased spending plans.

"But for the time being, we expect at most transitory inflation, that is what we expect coming out of a big recession," Cecilia Rouse, chair of the White House National Economic Council, also said in May 2021.[29]

Federal Reserve Chair Jerome Powell had said earlier, in March, that the trillions of dollars in Biden's America Rescue Plan would not lead to inflation, or okay, maybe just a bit!

"Our best view is that the effect on inflation will be neither particularly large nor persistent," Powell said. "And part of that just is that we've been living in a world of strong disinflationary pressures—around the world really—for a quarter of a century. We don't think that a one time surge in spending leading to temporary price increases would disrupt that."[30] Of course, it's easy to hold this view when you are paid by the taxpayer, you have a cushy job in D.C., and if inflation goes up, you just go to the taxpayer and make him pay you more money.

But the dangerous economic policies of Biden have continued to slam American taxpayers for over a year now. "Transitory" or "temporary" inflation sounds fancy

---

29 Doina Chiacu and Lisa Shumaker, "U.S. Treasury's Yellen tamps down inflation fears over Biden spending plan," Reuters, May 2, 2021, https://www.reuters.com/business/us-treasurys-yellen-tamps-down-inflation-fears-over-biden-spending-plan-2021-05-02/

30 Katherine Wiles, "Fed Chair: Rise in inflation not "particularly large" from $1.9 trillion rescue package," Marketplace, March 23, 2021, https://www.marketplace.org/2021/03/23/fed-chair-rise-in-inflation-not-particularly-large-from-1-9-trillion-rescue-package/

at D.C. cocktail parties or in meetings of overpaid bureaucrats. But, for hard-working Americans, the higher price of gas to fill up their trucks or the higher prices of groceries is not an academic theory or a definition from a textbook—it's real-life pain.

But at least Yellen, after inflicting painful policies on patriotic Americans, admitted she made a mistake, but primarily in not saying it in a better way.

"The American Rescue Plan was sized to do that, and it accomplished that mission," Yellen told *Bloomberg News* in February 2022.

"The Treasury chief argued that other countries with much weaker economies than the U.S. are also dealing with high inflation. That suggests, she said, that most of the rise in inflation was due to a shift in demand from services to goods and to disturbances in the supply of goods caused by Covid-19," *Bloomberg* reported.

"I think people heard 'transitory,' and to them it meant a couple of months," she said. "Maybe a better word could have been chosen." *Bloomberg* noted that Powell, with the Federal Reserve, backtracked on the word's use in November 2021.[31]

31 Christopher Condon, "Yellen Puts Inflation Blame Elsewhere, Defends Biden Stimulus," BQ Prime, February 3, 2022, https://www.bloombergquint.com/onweb/yellen-puts-inflation-blame-elsewhere-defends-biden-stimulus

What others are saying about Biden

- President Biden and his leftist pals talk about trusting the science and the experts. But what about the words of economists, financial analysts, and others who understand how the economy works? What have they said about Biden's policies?

Here's a sampling:

- A February 16, 2022, opinion piece in *The Hill* by Desmond Lachman predicted that the president would talk about his massive spending bills in the State of the Union but not the consequences. "Biden is almost certain to be less vocal about the serious inflation problem that has been unleashed by the powerful combination of the largest peacetime budget stimulus on record, the easiest of Federal Reserve monetary policies and a series of COVID-19-related supply-side problems," Lachman wrote. He is a researcher with the American Enterprise Institute and also worked as an economic strategist and in policy development for the International Monetary Fund. "In particular, he is likely to gloss over the fact that the economy is now experiencing its fastest inflation rate in the past 40 years. He also certainly will not mention that the 7.5 percent rate of consumer price inflation is resulting in wage declines in inflation-adjusted terms."[32]

- Kevin Hassett, a former Trump administration economist, said in February 2022 that it was obvious much earlier that inflation would skyrocket under Biden's plans. "It's obvious to a person who does macroeconomic modeling of the modern variety that inflation was going to take off," Hassett told CNBC.[33]
- Former Obama economic adviser Jason Furman previously warned about inflation. He said in November 2021 that the Federal Reserve "has been a little bit behind the curve," on inflation. "While he supported President Obama's Covid financial relief plan, Furman told CNBC the plan 'was larger than it needed to be' and that has played a role in the inflation now being experienced in the economy," the news site reported.[34]

---

32 Desmond Lachman, "The economic consequences of Joe Biden," *The Hill*, February 16, 2022, https://thehill.com/opinion/finance/594499-the-economic-consequences-of-joe-biden

33 Kayla Tausche, "Fed influence, shaky forecasts, delayed decisions: How the Biden administration misread the inflation threat," CNBC, February 4, 2022, https://www.cnbc.com/2022/02/04/how-the-biden-administration-misread-the-inflation-threat.html

34 Eric Rosenbaum, "Fed 'behind the curve' on inflation, says former Obama economist Jason Furman," CNBC, November 10, 2021, https://www.cnbc.com/2021/11/10/fed-behind-curve-on-inflation-former-obama-economist-jason-furman.html

- Former Bill Clinton Treasury Secretary Larry Summers has tried flagging inflation concerns for months now, apparently to no avail to the Biden administration. "I think policy is rather overdoing it," Summers said in May 2021. "The sense of serenity and complacency being projected by the economic policymakers, that this is all something that can easily be managed, is misplaced." "We're taking very substantial risks on the inflation side," he warned on May 18, 2021. "We are printing money, we are creating government bonds, we are borrowing on unprecedented scales," Summers warned. "Those are things that surely create more of a risk of a sharp dollar decline than we had before. And sharp dollar declines are much more likely to translate themselves into inflation than they were historically."[35]
- Former Obama Treasury Secretary Steven Rattner also criticized Biden's dangerous economic policies. He said it is "dishonest" for Biden to blame supply chain issues for inflation. Rattner made the comments in a February 17, 2022, opinion piece for the *New York Times*. "The reason for the inflation is the

35 Matt Egan, "Larry Summers sends stark inflation warning to Joe Biden," CNN, May 27, 2021, https://www.cnn.com/2021/05/26/economy/inflation-larry-summers-biden-fed/index.html

> supply chains were cut off," Biden told NBC News in February 2022. "Well, no. That's both simplistic and misleading," Rattner wrote. "For starters, the supply chains have not been 'cut off,' just stretched. And supply issues are by no means the root cause of our inflation. Blaming inflation on supply lines is like complaining about your sweater keeping you too warm after you've added several logs to the fireplace." Rattner said most of the problems come from an "overstimulated economy."[36]

Lachman, the economist, was right about his State of the Union address. Biden blamed the "pandemic" for the disruption. But many warehouses and factories continued to operate throughout the government coronavirus lockdowns. "Look, our economy roared back faster than almost anyone predicted, but the pandemic meant that businesses had a hard time hiring enough people because of the pandemic to keep up production in their factories. So, you didn't have people making those beams that went into buildings because they were out—the factory was closed," Biden incredibly claimed.[37]

---

36 Steven Rattner, "Biden Keeps Blaming the Supply Chain for Inflation. That's Dishonest," *New York Times*, February 17, 2022, https://www.nytimes.com/2022/02/17/opinion/inflation-supply-chain.html?referringSource=articleShare

37 "President Biden's State of the Union Address," The White House, March 1, 2022, https://www.whitehouse.gov/state-of-the-union-2022/

While Biden said he wants to make more things here and bring down costs, his reckless energy policies have made that more difficult. You cannot power American manufacturing right now on solar and wind power.

Secretary Rattner said the Biden administration needs to be "honest" about the causes of inflation.

"For its part, the White House needs to be more honest as it rolls out initiatives. It has promised robust antitrust enforcement, but while that is long overdue, it will have no discernible impact on competition or prices for years," he said. "And the high prices of meat and hearing aids, both of which Mr. Biden has vowed to address, are not at the heart of the current problem."

Rattner took Biden to task for claiming that the massive Build Back Better plan won't cost anything and thus won't add to the deficit.

"His Build Back Better plan claims to be deficit neutral, but that assertion is made credible only by using the fuzziest math. Over the first five years, the plan would add about $750 billion to the deficit, according to an analysis of the Congressional Budget Office's estimates," Rattner said. "With this year's fiscal gap estimated at $1.3 trillion, any new version of the plan should reduce the deficit substantially in its early years using honest math."[38]

And inflation definitely has hurt average Americans, who are paying more for gas, groceries, and other goods.

---

38 "CBO Scores the Build Back Better Act," Committee for a Responsible Federal Budget, December 17, 2021, https://www.crfb.org/blogs/cbo-scores-build-back-better-act

BizPacReview provided a good summary in February 2022. (Who knows how bad it will be when you read this book!) It reported on the United States' dropping on the Heritage Foundation's index of economic freedom based on Biden's liberal policies.

"The Index of Economic Freedom was launched in 1995 and uses a variety of methods to evaluate countries on rule of law, government size, regulatory efficiency and open markets, while also examining specific categories such as property rights, judicial effectiveness, government integrity and tax burden," BizPacReview explains. "Dovetailed into that is the Producer Price Index, which gauges the prices paid for the goods used to make final products such as metals and lumber for frames, grains for cereal, and even the glue, foil and plastics used for packaging. An increase in nearly ten percent in what it costs to make and deliver products means Americans will continue to feel the drain on their bank accounts."[39]

"The average for year-over-year inflation before Biden took office was 1.5 percent. Simply put, consumers are now paying 7.5 percent more than they were last year and producers are paying 9.7 percent more to make their products," *BizPacReview* reported. Ouch!

---

39 Frank Webster, "Inflation comes in higher than expected as America's economic freedom ranking drops to new low," Business and Politics Review, February 15, 2022, https://www.bizpacreview.com/2022/02/15/inflation-comes-in-higher-than-expected-as-americas-economic-freedom-ranking-drops-to-new-low-1201296/

The high cost to producers means that, in the future, we should expect higher prices too. American families are struggling under the weight of the Biden economy. This is a stark departure from the Trump presidency, when jobs were widely available (and no one tried to force you to take a vaccine to get one), the border was secured, which means wages went up, but energy costs were low, meaning the cost of products stayed at an affordable rate.

Yet the Biden-Harris-Sanders agenda has gone full steam ahead running over average, hard-working Americans who just want to save for a house, buy a decent car, and provide for their families. Meanwhile, the fat cats in D.C. get rich.

The Washington Times predicted that the Biden economy could "crush" Democrats in the 2022 midterms, though. So hopefully we can restore some sanity—though, for many of you, hanging on for a few more months or for more time until Biden is out of office is easier said than done.

"You don't have to be a Republican to see it. Just crunch the numbers: U.S. inflation recently surged to a nearly 40-year high, rising 6.8% from a year ago—the fastest increase since 1982. Used car and truck prices are up 31% since last year. Energy costs are up 33.3% year-over-year. The cost of gasoline is up even more (58.1%) in a span of 12 months," Ted Harvey wrote for the conservative publication in January 2022. "Throw in a 6.1% food price increase, and you have the lowest level of American purchasing power in a generation. In politics, the equation is simple: You start with a crisis—in this case, inflation. If enough people worry about the crisis, they will blame the current leadership in Washington. And blame eventually becomes change."

"Public opinion suggests historic change is on the way. Nearly 90% of Americans are 'highly concerned' about inflation, with many planning to cut back on spending—a vicious cycle for a consumer-driven economy. The crisis has been clearly identified," Harvey said.

Do you agree? Biden must be seeing poll numbers on a daily basis. But will it matter?

Of course, the Biden administration will continue to pursue a far-left agenda of higher taxes, higher spending, and putting the concerns of climate change activists over those of millions of Americans who don't want to pay nine dollars per gallon for gas.

In classic Biden "divide and dangerous" tactics, he and Senator Elizabeth Warren decided to blame companies, like grocery stores, for the inflation.

But this is not truthful.

Investment banker warns about media manipulation of inflation numbers

Former investment banker Carol Roth explained how the liberal media tried to downplay the threat of inflation or say it would be temporary.

"Inflation has been one of many big lies of the last couple of years, an entirely predictable outcome of very concrete events. The Federal Reserve pumping trillions of dollars into the market was always going to have consequences," Roth wrote in a December 2021 opinion piece for Fox News.[40] "Add to that the federal stimulus spending, plus lockdowns and other government decisions disrupting the labor market and supply chains, and you have the perfect (and, again, entirely predictable) storm of more money chasing a decreased supply of goods and services. You don't need an economics degree to surmise that higher prices would be the outcome."

She reminded readers how the Biden White House tried to say that, actually, the Fourth of July was cheaper in 2021—but, even with their own handpicked metrics, the total savings amounted to sixteen cents.

But the media tried to spin a story along with the political class, Roth said.

"Like when White House tried to tout the fictional 16 cents you were supposed to save on your Fourth of July cookout, or the recent tweet by the Democratic Congressional Campaign Committee that praised President Biden for a two cent decrease in gas prices after a large cost run-up," Roth said.

"And then, of course, if you weren't persuaded by any of the above, politicos from Sen. Elizabeth Warren, D-Mass., to White House Press Secretary Jen Psaki blame 'corporate greed' for the pricing run up, as if it now just

40 Carol Roth, "Inflation is real. So why is the liberal media still lying about it?," Fox News, December 15, 2021, https://www.foxnews.com/opinion/inflation-real-liberal-media-lying-carol-roth

occurred [to] companies to be 'greedy' and increase prices substantially," the banker wrote.

The bottom line is that the people in charge of multitrillion-dollar decisions are either wildly incompetent or liars themselves. No matter which one it is, or the way the media tries to spin it, the outcome is the same, and every American is paying dearly for it," she concluded.

High cost of manufacturing hurts Americans

Through the first year and more of the Biden White House, we've seen inflation, in every metric, increase. A few examples will suffice to show how the White House has let inflation run out of control and how regular, hard-working Americans are suffering and will continue to suffer.

For example, Texas manufacturers will likely see increased costs, which mean increased prices for consumers in 2022 and beyond due to higher costs for raw material. "The measure of prices for raw material in the Texas Manufacturing Outlook Survey, a key measure of state manufacturing conditions, rose to 82.1, with 83.6 percent of manufacturers saying materials cost more than a month earlier, 14.9 percent reporting no change, and just 1.5 percent reporting that prices had fallen," *Breitbart* reported in November 2021. "The six-month expectations index for raw materials prices moved up to 56.4, with 62.1 percent of manufacturers expecting higher costs. The finished goods price expectations index moved to 49.5, an 8.9 point jump, with 55.2 percent of manufactures expecting to raise their prices," *Breitbart* explained in its analysis of the survey results. Put in simple terms, the cost of inputs is going up, so the cost of the output, the final product, is going to continue to rise.

Texas executives, the people who are looking at the numbers, trying to get a hold on their finances and the economic outlook, explained some of the reasons. "Democrats are in control, so our buying power is declining. Spend, spend, spend, spend, spend is all they know, and what they spend it on hurts the working-class American," one executive said. "The vaccine mandate makes our employee outlook grim. We have many employees who are not willing (or not able) to be vaccinated and do not want to drive 30 minutes out of town for a weekly test. We are already having a difficult time finding people who want to work; now it is that much more difficult," another said. They were speaking about the now-defunct OSHA vaccine mandate.

Yet Biden continues to pursue unethical and illegal vaccine mandates through the government while also prodding businesses to do the same. A skeptic, like myself, would say that this seems to be a pretext for importing millions of foreign nationals to come here and compete with Americans for jobs, while bringing in their cultures and values at odds with American principles.

CHAPTER 2

FLOOD THE BORDER FROM THE SOUTH, FLY IN AFGHAN REFUGEES

President Trump spent four years doing the best he could to protect our border from criminal migrants and low-educated workers who would take jobs from Americans. He also sought to crack down on visa abuse and deport people who overstayed. He did the best he could to build hundreds of miles of border wall and use National Guard troops to protect America. He had to deal with renegade, activist judges, the ACLU, and other well-funded leftist interests, but overall he at least sent a message: Don't come here if you are not given permission to.

In a year, the Biden-Harris team has encouraged mass illegal migration tacitly, while making our neighborhoods less safe by flying migrants all around the country, sometimes in the middle of night. They also brought in tens of thousands of Afghan refugees, many of whom did not fight alongside U.S. troops. Within days, some were already allegedly committing horrific crimes, including rape.

Mark Morgan, the former acting commissioner of Customs and Border Patrol (CBP), explained how the administration did this in an analysis piece for the *New York Post* in January 2022.[41] He is also a national security fellow with the Heritage Foundation, which republished his article.

"Biden Encourages Massive Illegal Immigration and Tries To Hide It With Secret Flights," Morgan said.

He was discussing the secret flights of illegal migrants into states like Florida and Pennsylvania in the middle of the night. The free tickets, paid for by you and me, implicitly told them not to worry about coming to their trial date; welcome to America!

"The Biden administration doesn't want media attention on illegal immigration, its open border policies, or the results of those policies. How do we know? A security officer just said so, in an explosive video of secretive, dark-of-night flights transporting illegal immigrants to various points throughout the U.S," Morgan explained. "This video merits coast-to-coast media coverage, not just to expose the administration's stealth operations that flout the laws, but to encourage Americans and leaders at all

41 Lora Ries and Mark Morgan, "Biden Encourages Massive Illegal Immigration and Tries to Hide It With Secret Flights," The Heritage Foundation, January 31, 2022, https://www.heritage.org/immigration/commentary/biden-encourages-massive-illegal-immigration-and-tries-hide-it-secret

levels of government to demand that the administration start protecting our border, our country, and our citizens."

"Over the last several months, night flights of illegal migrants have been periodically reported in places such as Florida, New York, Pennsylvania and Tennessee. In each instance, state and local officials received no notice they were coming, let alone given an option to refuse them admission. The administration has no apparent concern with how these 'air lifts' may burden local officials with additional costs and facilities capacity in areas such as education, housing, healthcare and law enforcement," Morgan wrote.

Our dangerous and divisive President Biden, along with his Homeland Security Secretary Alejandro Mayorkas, amplified fake news vitriol at brave Border Patrol agents, falsely claiming they were "whipping" Haitian migrants. Now these agents were not in fact "whipping" anyone; they had reins on horses. But let's ask another question—how did Haitian migrants end up at our southern border? Or, for that matter, how did two-thousand Romanians end up at the U.S.-Mexico border? Doesn't matter to Biden-Harris—just get them here and signed up for welfare.

A national security reporter offers this great insight: Migrants from around the world are traveling here because they believe, and correctly so, that they'll at least be able to stay here through the end of the Biden administration. And history tells us that, once they have been here a few years, it will almost be impossible to get rid of these criminal migrants. "This guy is a hard worker!" the leftists will cry. "Really, you're going to deport a 70-year-old grandma?"

"Roma migrants from Europe are funneling across the U.S.-Mexico border and onto the shores of a tiny river-front town, making them the latest group of migrants to flock to America since President Joe Biden took office in January," Anna Giaritelli, national security reporter for the *Washington Examiner*, wrote in May 2021. "The rising number of non-Latin American people showing up at the southern border has become a trend as groups from Europe and South America take bigger risks in hopes of being admitted to the United States since the Biden administration relaxed immigration protocols."[42]

"Many of the European migrants are flying into Mexico from Europe because Mexico does not require visitors to obtain a visa before entering the country. From Mexico, the migrants travel to the U.S.-Mexico border and make their way through the border river in south Texas, where Border Patrol agents on the U.S. side will take them into custody," she explained further. "People who make asylum claims will not be turned away at the border despite a public health order in effect that states all illegal crossers ought to be returned across the border."

That was in May 2021, before Afghan refugees, many healthy men who refused to defend their homeland and instead fled to America, were airlifted here with minimal

42 Anna Giaritelli, "Roma migrants follow trend of non-Latin American people showing up at border," *Washington Examiner*, May 26, 2021, https://www.washingtonexaminer.com/news/roma-migrants-trend-non-latin-american-people-border

vetting during the botched pullout from Afghanistan. It didn't take long for these refugees to come here and begin committing crimes.

"An Afghan refugee housed at the Quantico, Virginia, Marine Corps base after he fled the country has been convicted by a federal jury with a sexual assault," the Associated Press reported in January 2022. "[Mohammed] Tariq was arrested in September at Camp Upshur in Quantico, Virginia, after Marines observed him fondling the girl, who was not related to him, above her clothes on her private parts.

"According to court papers, Tariq tried to explain through interpreters that his conduct was acceptable in his culture. Efforts to have his statements suppressed were rejected by the judge."

Tariq "was brought to Virginia after working alongside U.S. troops in Afghanistan," the AP reported.[43]

He shouldn't be confused with Zabihullah Muhmand, another refugee from Afghanistan. "The Missoula [Montana] Police Department told Fox that Zabihullah Muhmand was arrested after they received a 911 call from the victim and a local motel about concerning behavior," Fox News

---

43 "Afghan refugee convicted of assaulting girl, 3, at Quantico Marine Base," *Air Force Times*, January 25, 2022, https://www.airforcetimes.com/news/2022/01/25/afghan-refugee-convicted-of-assaulting-girl-3-at-quantico-marine-base/?contentQuery=%7B%22section%22%3A%22%2Fhome%22%2C%22exclude%22%3A%22%2Fnews%22%2C%22from%22%3A15%2C%22size%22%3A10%7D&contentFeatureId=f0fmoahPVC2AbfL-2-1-8

reported.[44] Muhmand, 19, is now being held at the Missoula County Jail on charges of sexual intercourse without consent, and the case is being investigated by detectives—who did not confirm his evacuee status. The local court told Fox News that there is a federal hold on Muhmand.

"These unvetted Afghans do not share our culture and our values, and as this horrific incident shows they represent a serious risk to our communities," Republican Representative Matt Rosendale said. "We cannot allow this administration to continue to jeopardize the safety of our communities and the security of our nation in the name of empathy."

Nor should Muhmand be confused with two other refugees placed in Wisconsin.

"Bahrullah Noori, 20, is charged with one count of attempting to engage in a sex act with a minor by force and three counts of engaging in a sex act with a minor. One of the latter counts also alleges the use of force. Investigators say both of Noori's alleged victims were under the age of 16," the *New York Post* reported in September 2021.

"The second indictment charges 32-year-old Mohammad Haroon Imaad with assaulting his wife on Sept. 7 by strangling and suffocating her," the *New York Post* reported. "A complaint states that Imaad's wife claimed to

44 Adam Shaw and Aishah Hasnie, "Afghan evacuee charged with rape in Montana, governor says, demanding resettlement halt," Fox News, October 21, 2021, https://www.foxnews.com/politics/afghan-refugee-charged-rape-montana-governor-demands-resettlement-halt

soldiers through an interpreter that her husband had also struck their children on 'multiple occasions' and alleged that he 'beat me many times in Afghanistan to the point I lost vision in both eyes.'"

Leftists will say that we need to let in all these Afghans. A researcher with the Center for Immigration Studies explained how there were some specific ways that refugees who actually helped American troops could be let in—actual, patriotic people who could receive the full backing of our brave men and women in uniform. But Biden wanted to bring in many, many more, way beyond any sort of responsibility we might have.

"[T]here are millions of Afghans who did not assist U.S. forces, but who could nonetheless end up wanting to leave their country as refugees, fearful of a Taliban rule. (Afghanistan's population is about thirty-eight million.) The United States cannot possibly welcome millions of potential Afghan refugees," Nayla Rush wrote.[45]

"There must be a limit to the United States' capacity (not to mention will) to admit people in need. Can we welcome in all: border crossers from Central America (and other countries), Afghans, earthquake survivors, and, as per President Biden's plan, 'climate refugees'? Where does the United States government draw the line?" Rush asked.

More information on the backgrounds of some of these refugees hastily flown into the United States con-

---

45 Nayla Rush, "How Many Afghans Should We Admit?," Center for Immigration Studies, August 24, 2021, https://cis.org/Rush/How-Many-Afghans-Should-We-Admit

tinues to come to light, and as time goes by, the decision by the Biden administration seems worse and worse every day. *Just the News* reported in February 2022 that the Pentagon, whose primary focus is keeping America safe, let in fifty Afghans who pose "serious security risks."[46] The Pentagon Inspector General's report stated that twenty-eight of thirty-one refugees with "derogatory information," meaning red flags that should have stopped them from entering the country, cannot be located.[47] So at least twenty-eight criminal and/or violent refugees who come from a place with a much different culture than ours could be anywhere in the United States—is this incompetence or not? These people could be anywhere, mixing in with the thousands of illegal migrants Biden has spread across the country in just the past year.

"Afghan evacuees were not vetted by the [National Counterterrorism Center] using all DoD data prior to arriving in [the United States]," the IG report said. *Refugees were not vetted using our Department of Defense (DOD) database.* Is every single refugee going to be a criminal? No, of course not. But it is the duty of the Commander-in-Chief to keep us safe, and in the rush to get refugees

46 John Solomon, "Biden Pentagon let 50 Afghans posing serious security risks into the United States, watchdog finds," *Just the News*, February 19, 2022, https://justthenews.com/government/security/biden-pentagon-mistakenly-let-50-afghans-serious-security-risks-united-states

47 Inspector General, US Department of Defense, "Evaluation of the Screening of Displaced Persons from Afghanistan" (Report, Virginia, 2022), 1–34, https://media.defense.gov/2022/Feb/17/2002940841/-1/-1/1/DODIG-222-065.PDF

over here or to avoid the scenes of Taliban killing Afghans, the Biden administration pursued its trademark wokeness and liberal agenda at the expense of the safety of Americans. The report notes that a lot of work was done to quickly process refugees to get them work authorizations and other papers.

"As a result of the NCTC not vetting Afghan evacuees against all available data, the United States faces potential security risks if individuals with derogatory information are allowed to stay in the country. In addition, the U.S. Government could mistakenly grant [Special Immigrant Visa] or parolee status to ineligible Afghan evacuees with derogatory information gathered from the DoD...database," the Inspector General warned.

Too bad the refugees weren't wearing Make America Great Again hats; then at least the DOD would have gone all out to keep a close eye on them and make sure they weren't terrorists—because the priority of the DOD and the Department of Homeland Security has become to laser focus on the supposed threat from right-wingers or "white supremacists" or gun owners, Christians, etc.

After all, it was the Biden administration that sought to crack down on conservative evangelicals and Catholics as the real threat in the American military, according to a First Amendment attorney and Marine reservist. He also is a Pentagon advisor and said the DOD is pursuing "wokeness."

"Instead of monitoring external threats, the Pentagon is on a mission to identify and remove whomever it labels as extremists from America's armed forces," Mike Berry warned in June 2021 in the *Washington Examiner*. "But the Pentagon is now poised to expand upon that definition to include constitutionally protected speech."[48]

He gave the example of an Army chaplain forced out because he criticized the inclusion of gender-confused men and women in the military. Berry previously "warned that the First Amendment rights of service members, particularly Catholic and evangelical soldiers, could be at risk," the *Washington Examiner* reported in March 2021.[49]

"The U.S. Army produced training materials that labeled evangelical Christians and Catholics as religious extremists alongside Hamas and al Qaeda, never mind the fact that evangelicals and Catholics continue to comprise the majority of those serving in uniform today," Berry said. "Labeling religious or political beliefs that are held by tens of millions of Americans as extremists is to declare them unwelcome and unfit to serve is to say, 'Uncle Sam does not want you.'"

That's where the focus of the woke DOD is. It's too bad it cannot focus on its primary goal of protecting the American homeland and stopping the flow of illegal migrants into the country.

---

48 Mike Berry, "Wokeness warriors take over the Pentagon," *Washington Examiner*, June 19, 2021, https://www.washingtonexaminer.com/opinion/wokeness-warriors-take-over-the-pentagon

49 Abraham Mahshie, "Conservatives fear extremism in military debate is 'political theater' to target Christians," *Washington Examiner*, March 24, 2021, https://www.washingtonexaminer.com/policy/defense-national-security/conservatives-fear-extremism-military-debate-political-theater-target-christians

Immigrant crime

Law enforcement will have its hands full with trying to manage the criminal activity from the flood of migrants that are coming through our border every day. The Biden administration, as I write this, is moving thousands of single men throughout the country without any clear plan to ever send them back to their home country.

Footage captured by Fox News in January and February 2022 shows a mass group of single, young men being released into the United States in Texas.

"Several of the migrants told Fox that they had crossed illegally that morning, paying approximately $2,000 per person to cartel smugglers. They also said they were flying to destinations including Miami, Houston and Atlanta," Fox News reported. As noted by Fox, President Trump had used Title 42 to expel those likely to become a burden on the taxpayer. While a judge ordered the Biden administration to keep it in place, the Department of Homeland Security has basically ignored it. "Single adults are typically being expelled via Trump-era Title 42 public health protections. The Biden administration kept Title 42 in place but is not applying it to unaccompanied children or most migrant families. However, single adults have long been the easiest category of migrant to deport," Fox noted.

The illegal and dangerous operations by the Biden administration have reportedly been going on since spring 2021, just shortly after the Biden-Harris team took office. Once the message goes out that you can come here and get a free ticket to a nice place like Miami or Houston, thousands and thousands more illegal migrants will travel to our country. Meanwhile, hard-working Americans have to pick up the taxpayer slack for the increased cost on communities and on the welfare system.

"[An] Immigration and Customs Enforcement agent, who's involved in the migrant release operation, said it's been going on discreetly since the spring, Fox News reported. The unidentified official said some of the migrants who've been released have criminal records for misdemeanors including assault, drunken driving, drug possession and illegal re-entry," correspondent Bill Melugin said.[50] This is, frankly, despicable and dangerous. Imagine that you have worked hard your whole life to buy a nice house in a safe neighborhood, you weathered the pandemic, and then the Biden administration ships criminal young men to your neighborhood to commit crime, live on welfare, and cause other problems. Every one of these criminal migrants, and they are all criminal by virtue of coming here illegally, should immediately be expelled.

The cost to taxpayers is enormous. Jason Richwine, with the Center for Immigration Studies, presents one example of how Florida has been saddled with the cost of illegal immigration—and this was before Biden opened the floodgates further to the entire world.

---

50 Callie Patteson, Bruce Golding and Carl Campanile, "Migrants with criminal records among those being released in the US: ICE agent," *New York Post*, January 27, 2022, https://nypost.com/2022/01/27/migrants-with-criminal-records-among-those-being-released-in-the-us-ice-agent/

"Although illegal immigration poses many challenges, the increase in state expenditures is perhaps the most immediate one. In a recent report for the Center for Immigration Studies, I calculated that Florida spent approximately $2 billion in 2019 on major health and education programs for the nearly 800,000 immigrants who lived in the state illegally before the recent surge," Richwine wrote in the *Tallahassee Democrat* in January 2022.[51]

"But aren't those living in the country illegally barred from receiving public benefits? This is a common misconception," he said. "Although most of those entering the country illegally cannot directly receive welfare, the state still supports them in other ways, especially through their children. For example, Florida spent an estimated $52 million on Medicaid coverage for births to immigrants who arrived illegally in 2019, and another $148 million on Medicaid coverage for their older U.S.-born children."

Those are your taxpayer dollars. You work hard, putting in forty, fifty, sixty hours a week to provide for yourself and your family. You're okay paying taxes to support the local police and firefighters and a social safety net for when someone truly cannot work because they became disabled, maybe as a veteran or while working on the front lines. You're okay with federal taxes, even if they're a bit high, when it goes to providing free med-

---

51 Jason Richwine, "DeSantis is right about the cost of illegal immigration | Opinion," *Tallahassee Democrat*, January 24, 2022, https://www.tallahassee.com/story/opinion/2022/01/24/desantis-right-cost-illegal-immigration-opinion/6607558001/

ical care for our veterans or funds basic infrastructure. But your government now takes that money and spends it on illegal migrants, many of whom are not fleeing any sort of real political violence but just want to come live in America but refuse to follow the rules and come here legally.

Criminal activity of migrants

It's one issue if the cost from illegal migration were purely fiscal—increased spending on healthcare, education, and other areas because many of these migrants are not highly educated and will need Medicaid insurance.

But many of these migrants also commit crimes here *and before even entering the country*. That's right. When we talk about immigrant crime, it's not someone who came here when they were five and then twenty years later they turn out to be a criminal. Some people are coming to this country *with criminal records*.

"U.S. Border Patrol Agents in the El Paso sector in the last seven days have encountered numerous migrants with criminal records and gang affiliations," the CBP announced in February 2022.

"The El Paso Sector continues to see migrants with criminal records attempting to enter our borders with different criminal backgrounds that include assault, burglary, driving under the influence, homicide, illegal drug possession, illegal weapon possession and sexual offenses," the CBP said. "Since the beginning of the fiscal year 2022, agents have encountered more than 244 migrants with previous criminal records."[52]

In November 2021, the CBP arrested criminal migrants *who had previously been deported.* "Big Bend Sector Border Patrol agents apprehended a large group of migrants near Alpine, Texas, including several previously deported criminal aliens. Those arrested included a deported rapist and a drug trafficker," *Breitbart* reported.[53]

"Criminal records indicate a California court in Santa Clara County convicted [one of the migrants] for Rape by Force/Fear and Obstruction/Resisting Officer in 2000," officials stated. The court sentenced the man to three years in prison, and ICE Enforcement and Removal Operations officers removed him from the United States.

"Agents removed 67 migrants from the dangerous compartment, officials stated. They identified the 67 migrants as citizens of El Salvador (3), Guatemala (19), Honduras (4), and Mexico (41)," *Breitbart* reported. These arrests weren't a fluke or just a case of a few bad hombres.

"Rio Grande Valley Sector Border Patrol (RGV) agents arrested a migrant previously convicted of possession of child pornography and a Mara-Salvatrucha (MS-13) gang

---

52 "El Paso Sector continues to encounter migrants with criminal records," U.S. Customs and Border Protection, February 1, 2022, https://www.cbp.gov/newsroom/local-media-release/el-paso-sector-continues-encounter-migrants-criminal-records

53 Bob Price, "Deported Rapist, Criminal Migrants, Found in Large Migrant Group near Border in West Texas," *Breitbart*, November 11, 2021, https://www.breitbart.com/border/2021/11/11/deported-rapist-criminal-migrants-found-in-large-migrant-group-near-border-in-west-texas/

member," CBP announced in November 2021. "On Oct. 29, Brownsville Border Patrol Station agents apprehended a group of seven migrants in Brownsville. Record checks on Fredy Flores-Galeana, a Mexican national, revealed he was convicted of possession of child pornography and was sentenced to two years confinement. He was later sentenced to 26 months confinement by an immigration judge and subsequently removed from the United States," the CBP announced. "On Oct. 30, RGV agents apprehended a group of 11 migrants near Raymondville. Record checks on a Honduran national, revealed he is a MS-13 gang member. In 2008, he was convicted of accommodating sale, possession of a controlled substance, and possession with intent to distribute cocaine in Virginia. He was sentenced to five years incarceration for each of the charges and was subsequently removed from the United States."[54]

But these weren't the only ones. "Fiscal year 2021, Border Patrol agents around the nation arrested 10,763 criminal migrants, of those, more than 1,900 were arrested in the RGV."

Again, we might be a little more sympathetic to someone who came here with a clean record, as far as we can tell, with a legitimate fear of political violence. But what about when we *know* someone is a criminal, that *they are accused of committing a vicious crime*, and we still let them stay?

---

54 Roger Maier, "Criminal Migrants Arrested in the RGV," US Customs and Border Protection, November 1, 2021, https://www.cbp.gov/newsroom/local-media-release/criminal-migrants-arrested-rgv

"Adrienne Sophia Exum died in a north Houston crash in November 2020 when the car she was driving was hit by a pickup truck driver, Heriberto Fuerte-Padilla, according to KTRK-TV. She was ejected from her car and died at the scene," the *Independent Journal Review* (*IJR*) reported.[55] "Police said Fuerte-Padilla was drunk at the time of the crash and tried to run away from police after the accident."

So immediately he was deported back to his home country, right? Wrong. "In the closing days of the Trump administration, Fuerte-Padilla, who was in the country illegally, was marked for deportation," the *IJR* reported. "But now, as the Department of Homeland Security and Immigration and Customs Enforcement implement new Biden administration rules designed to reduce the number of deportations, Fuerte-Padilla is no longer up for deportation, according to the Washington Times."

So, if criminal migrants can stay here, and we bring in refugees who then commit crimes, who does the Biden administration focus its ire on? Well, we found out that its targets include people who showed up at school board meetings and protested COVID mandates or curriculum they found inappropriate. It includes one parent who came to speak out against the cover-up of the rape of his daughter. That's who the Biden administration, along with

---

55 Jack Davis, "Biden's ICE Cancels Deportation Order for Illegal Immigrant Accused of Killing Teen Girl in Drunken Hit-and-Run," *Independent Journal Review*, January 31, 2022, https://ijr.com/bidens-ice-cancels-deportation-order-illegal-immigrant-accused/

his supposedly moderate, neutral AG Merrick Garland, decided to sic the FBI and federal prosecutors on—until they were caught and the targeting blew up in their faces.

It's no wonder that a former top Department of Justice (DOJ) official said the Biden administration is hurting Americans' trust.

"For all of his rhetoric, and for all of his talk about returning the Department of Justice to norms and all of those other such things, Merrick Garland's Department of Justice has betrayed the trust of the American people," Gene Hamilton told *Just the News* in February 2022. "This Department of Justice has just completely gone to the left, completely done the opposite of returning to norms," he said. "If that is such a thing. And they're really doing the bidding of the radical left these days." Hamilton previously worked for Trump-era Attorneys General William Barr and Jeff Sessions.

Hamilton told *Just the News* that efforts by the Biden administration to stop election integrity laws in Georgia and Texas as well as the targeting of parents at school boards were two key examples.

"There's chains of approval, and different things that usually happen when you're going to issue a memo of that significance," he said. "But with Garland's memo, it clearly did not go through the ordinary course. It clearly was precooked, prebaked." As we will see now, Gene Hamilton is absolutely correct.

CHAPTER 3

THE WHITE HOUSE COORDINATES WITH SCHOOL BOARD GROUP TO COMPARE ACTIVIST PARENTS TO DOMESTIC TERRORISTS

The Biden-Harris team does not have time to enforce immigration law in the United States. AG Merrick Garland could use the DOJ to send a clear message to illegal immigrants by ordering federal prosecutors to ramp up prosecutions for illegal border crossing or having them prosecute people who violate federal law and overstay their visas. The Department of Homeland Security could use National Guard troops, as Trump did, and position them on the southern border. But, instead, the national security apparatus and federal prosecutors, according to disgraced AG Merrick Garland, should be focused on targeting parents who show up at school board meetings to protest mask mandates or curriculum.

In a stunning display of DOJ overreach, and in the age of the FBI's targeting of Trump and his allies, that's saying something; the National School Boards Association (NSBA) coordinated with senior Biden administration officials to ask that parents and other activists be treated as domestic terrorists. If you don't know about the NSBA, you'd probably assume that one of their primary federal goals would be to secure funding for schools, perhaps getting money to put in better air filters to prevent the transmission of COVID.

But, in fact, senior NSBA leadership, along with the Biden administration, sought to use the power of the federal government to crack down on...moms and dads who didn't want their kids to be forced to wear a mask eight hours a day or be forced to read pornographic homosexual propaganda. Or who opposed the teaching of racist and divisive Critical Race Theory (CRT).

NSBA President Viola Garcia and Executive Director Chip Slaven, in a letter we now know was not sent after a majority vote of school boards, begged for federal surveillance of patriotic Americans who were exercising their First Amendment rights.

"America's public schools and its education leaders are under an immediate threat. The National School Boards

Association (NSBA) respectfully asks for federal law enforcement and other assistance to deal with the growing number of threats of violence and acts of intimidation occurring across the nation," the letter said. "Local school board members want to hear from their communities on important issues and that must be at the forefront of good school board governance and promotion of free speech. However, there also must be safeguards in place to protect public schools and dedicated education leaders as they do their jobs."[56]

The letter continued on to claim, falsely, that CRT is not taught in public schools. "Coupled with attacks against school board members and educators for approving policies for masks to protect the health and safety of students and school employees, many public school officials are also facing physical threats because of propaganda purporting the false inclusion of critical race theory within classroom instruction and curricula," the September 29, 2021, letter said. "This propaganda continues despite the fact that critical race theory is not taught in public schools and remains a complex law school and graduate school subject well beyond the scope of a K-12 class."

The letter went on to ask the federal government to use all laws at its disposal, including the 9/11-era PATRIOT Act.

56 NSBA to President Biden, "Re: Federal Assistance to Stop Threats and Acts of Violence Against Public Schoolchildren, Public School Board Members, and Other Public School District Officials and Educators," September 29, 2021, https://www.documentcloud.org/documents/21094557-national-school-boards-association-letter-to-biden

"NSBA specifically solicits the expertise and resources of the U.S. Department of Justice, Federal Bureau of Investigation (FBI), U.S. Department of Homeland Security, U.S. Secret Service, and its National Threat Assessment Center regarding the level of risk to public schoolchildren, educators, board members, and facilities/campuses," the anti-American NSBA wrote. "We also request the assistance of the U.S. Postal Inspection Service to intervene against threatening letters and cyberbullying attacks that have been transmitted to students, school board members, district administrators, and other educators. As these acts of malice, violence, and threats against public school officials have increased, the classification of these heinous actions could be the equivalent to a form of domestic terrorism and hate crimes."

Did you catch that last part? "Domestic terrorism." One of those domestic terrorists, we later learned, was a brave Virginia man who came to a school board meeting to criticize the rape cover-up of his teenage daughter by a cross-dressing boy. That boy was later moved to another school where he raped another girl.[57]

The school board association requested help from "the U.S. Departments of Justice, Education, and Homeland Security, along with the appropriate training, coordination, investigations, and enforcement mechanisms from

57 Gabe Kaminsky, "Loudoun Rapist Removed From Sex Offender Registry After County Board Member Says He's The Victim," *Daily Wire*, January 27, 2022, https://www.dailywire.com/news/loudoun-rapist-removed-from-sex-offender-registry-after-county-board-member-says-hes-the-victim

the FBI, including any technical assistance necessary from, and state and local coordination with, its National Security Branch and Counterterrorism Division, as well as any other federal agency with relevant jurisdictional authority and oversight."

"Additionally, NSBA requests that such review examine appropriate enforceable actions against these crimes and acts of violence under the Gun-Free School Zones Act, the PATRIOT Act in regards to domestic terrorism, the Matthew Shepard and James Byrd Jr. Hate Crimes Prevention Act, the Violent Interference with Federally Protected Rights statute, the Conspiracy Against Rights statute, [and] an Executive Order to enforce all applicable federal laws," against Americans, the letter said.

At least one district attorney heard the call to target parents and got to work writing up ways that Montana law enforcement could harass and criminally charge American citizens exercising their First Amendment rights to free speech and assembly.

In a memo that the *AP* obtained but did not publish, State's Attorney Leif Johnson informed law enforcement in the state what charges could be possible against parents.[58] Johnson suggested that Montana sheriffs and even the state's AG be on the lookout for ways to use federal *kidnapping* charges against parents. Other options

58 Renee Nal, "Montana Memo Revealed: DOJ Blueprint to Persecute and Intimidate Parents (Videos)," Rair Foundation, October 28, 2021, https://rairfoundation.com/montana-memo-revealed-doj-blueprint-to-persecute-and-intimidate-parents-videos/

included "cyberstalking," "false information and hoaxes," and "repeated phone calls."

We now know that this letter was not the result of a meeting of concerned education executives but came at the direction of Secretary of Education Miguel Cardona. That's right—a top-ranked federal official reached out to a school board association to solicit a letter that could then be used as a pretext to bring in federal law enforcement to spy on Americans. Let's be clear on something—if parents show up to school board meetings and do assault someone or send threatening messages, local law enforcement can handle what is essentially a harassment or trespassing charge. There's no need to bring in the FBI to handle a heated school board meeting.

"Newly released internal emails reveal that the National School Boards Association coordinated with the White House and the Department of Justice before sending President Biden the notorious letter that compared concerned parents to domestic terrorists," Fox News reported in November 2021.[59]Memos obtained by Parents Defending Education, a right-leaning advocacy and government transparency group, show that NSBA President Garcia was writing to members to talk about a White House meeting September 14, two weeks prior to the domestic terrorist letter being sent.

---

59 Tyler O'Neil, "NSBA coordinated with White House, DOJ before sending notorious 'domestic terrorists' letter: emails," Fox News, November 12, 2021, https://www.foxnews.com/politics/nsba-coordinated-with-white-house-doj-before-sending-notorious-domestic-terrorists-letter-emails

But AG Merrick Garland, once heralded as a moderate, fair-minded guy when Obama wanted him on the Supreme Court, had told the U.S. Senate that his own DOJ memorandum did not rely on the NSBA letter. "Citing an increase in harassment, intimidation and threats of violence against school board members, teachers and workers in our nation's public schools, today Attorney General Merrick B. Garland directed the FBI and U.S. Attorneys' Offices to meet in the next 30 days with federal, state, Tribal, territorial and local law enforcement leaders to discuss strategies for addressing this disturbing trend. These sessions will open dedicated lines of communication for threat reporting, assessment and response by law enforcement," a DOJ press release on October 4 said.[60]The related memo directed the FBI and federal prosecutors to "facilitate the discussion of strategies" for possible reporting and prosecution of American citizens.[61]

One wonders if Secretary Cardona discussed the call to target American individuals at a Cabinet meeting with Garland. "A newly released email indicates Education Secretary Miguel Cardona solicited last September's letter from the National School Boards Association which

---

60 "Justice Department Addresses Violent Threats Against School Officials and Teachers," Office of Public Affairs (Department of Justice), October 4, 2021, https://www.justice.gov/opa/pr/justice-department-addresses-violent-threats-against-school-officials-and-teachers

61 "Garland memo," *Marietta Daily Journal*, October 6, 2021, https://www.mdjonline.com/garland-memo/pdf_01521414-26b6-11ec-a064-ff37c7337c32.html

compared parents protesting at school board meetings to domestic terrorists," the *New York Post* reported in January 2022.[62] "In an Oct. 6 message to NSBA board member Marnie Maraldo, Secretary-Treasurer Kristi Swett said then-interim CEO Chip Slaven had told his fellow officers 'he was writing a letter to provide information to the White House, from a request by Secretary Cardona.'"

So, we now have proof that, at a minimum (and who knows what else will come out by the time you read this book), the NSBA met with White House officials and Secretary Cardona asked for more information from the NSBA.[63]

This is dangerous and divisive. Parents have every right to attend school board meetings and share their opinions on policies. In fact, you do not even have to be a parent—it is the right of every American taxpayer to comment on the way their local government entities are spending money and the policies they are putting into place. The good news is that the leftist NSBA has suffered massive losses due to its call to treat Americans as domestic terrorists.

State after state school board associations either distanced themselves from the NSBA or completely broke

---

62 Callie Patteson, "Email suggests Education Secretary Miguel Cardona asked for school board 'domestic terror' letter," *New York Post*, January 11, 2022, https://nypost.com/2022/01/11/miguel-cardona-asked-for-school-board-domestic-terror-letter/

63 I suggest you check out Parents Defending Education's website, where they regularly have posted updates on this situation and other matters: https://defendinged.org/newsroom/

away, depriving it of money. Both Republican and Democratic state associations cut ties with the leftist NSBA, including the Illinois Association of School Boards.

"To date, 26 state school boards associations have distanced themselves from the national association over the controversial letter," *The Center Square* reported in November 2021. "Of them, thirteen discontinued membership or stopped paying dues to it."[64]

The Illinois school board group specifically cited the domestic terrorism letter."IASB communicated to NSBA that 'IASB no longer believes that NSBA can fill this important role.' In September NSBA sent a letter to President Biden calling for federal assistance, without knowledge or support of its state association members," the letter said, according to *The Center Square*.

This is great news. Parents and activists should demand that their school boards are not funding subversive, anti-American activities such as those the NASB wants carried out against free Americans.

And what were so many of these parents concerned about? A racist ideology called Critical Race Theory, which holds that racism is at the center of everything in society—and, by extension, white people are to blame for all of the world's problems.

---

64 The Center Square Staff, "Illinois school board association ends membership with NSBA over parent-threat letter," *Just the News*, November 9, 2021, https://justthenews.com/nation/states/illinois-school-board-association-ends-membership-nsba-over-parent-threat-letter

CRT is a poison that has slowly, then quickly, been spreading across the country, but its roots go back to 20th-century German thinkers. "The origins of this ideology is an important question, for CRT has nothing to do with civil rights, or improving black lives or making them 'matter,'" Bruce Thornton explained in an article for *FrontPageMag*.[65] "CRT has its roots in Marxism, as one of the founders of BLM has bragged," Thornton said.

The Heritage Foundation explained that the roots of CRT are ultimately Marxist.

"The origins of Critical Theory can be traced to the 1937 manifesto of the Institute for Social Research in Frankfurt, colloquially known as the Frankfurt School. One of the first examples of what has come to be called the Western Marxist schools of thought, the Institute modeled itself on the Moscow-based Marx-Engels Institute," the Heritage Foundation said.

From the beginning, its proponents had to use neutral sounding names to cover up its true aims and confuse people so they do not understand what is happening.

"Originally, the school's official name was going to be the Institut fur Marxismus (Institute for Marxism), but, ever desirous of downplaying their Marxist roots, its founders thought it prudent to adopt a less provocative title, according to one of the best histories of the

65 Bruce Thornton, "Critical Race Theory's Marxist Roots," *Frontpage Mag*, June 10, 2021, https://www.frontpagemag.com/fpm/2021/06/critical-race-theorys-marxist-roots-bruce-thornton/

school's work and of Critical Theory itself, *The Dialectical Imagination*, by Martin Jay."[66]

While proponents initially, and still do, try to downplay its existence in public schools, it does exist in our schools and in the government, while telling you that we need to keep teaching about race and privilege. Leftists will try to tell you that CRT is just a law school theory or that you only learn about it in graduate-level social science courses—but that we need to have five-year-olds do privilege walks or force white kids to apologize to black kids! In fact, CRT infects our schools, and parents were right to get upset and speak out.

One person who knows that CRT infects our schools is AG Merrick Garland—because his son-in-law has a financial stake in a company that pushes CRT. Ahh! A conflict of interest that would make the Bidens blush—yes, the same AG Garland who wanted federal prosecutors to keep a close eye on the thirty-nine-year-old mom who wanted to know why her son had to read an Ibram X. Kendi book also has a daughter married to a CRT training company executive.

To make it simpler—Garland's family gets more money that more schools that use their training materials. The more parents that come to school board meetings and expose CRT, the fewer potential clients for the Garland family.

---

66 Jonathan Butcher and Mike Gonzalez, "Critical Race Theory," Heritage, https://www.heritage.org/sites/default/files/2020-12/BG3567.pdf

"The education company co-founded by Attorney General Merrick Garland's son-in-law is facing fresh scrutiny after it was revealed the company supports critical race theory curricula while servicing 23,000 schools in the nation, costing tax payers hundreds of thousands of dollars—while Garland cracks down on opposition to the ideology," the *New York Post* reported in October 2021.[67] "Panorama Education, co-founded by Xan Tanner, sells surveys to school districts nationwide with a focus on 'social and emotion climate,' according to a report by Forbes."

"According to OpenTheBooks, a government expenditure library, the company has been hired by school districts in California, Delaware, Florida, Georgia, Illinois, Indiana, Iowa, Maine, Massachusetts, Michigan, New Hampshire, New Mexico, North Carolina, Ohio, Oregon, Pennsylvania, Rhode Island, Texas, Utah, Virginia, and Wyoming for surveys or training," the *New York Post* reported.

So here's how it works. The company comes in and sends out a survey, which will likely find some sort of level of someone not feeling comfortable. In a school with fifty to one hundred employees, someone will say they are being mistreated—and, if you can prime them to think it's because of their race, all the better for the Garland family business.

---

67 Callie Patteson, "AG Garland's son-in-law's education company supports critical race theory," *New York Post*, October 13, 2021, https://nypost.com/2021/10/13/critical-race-theory-firm-linked-to-ag-garlands-kin-serves-schoolscompany-co-founded-by-ag-garlands-son-in-law-serves-over-20k-schools/

Then, Xan Tanner's company comes in and charges thousands and thousands of dollars to put the school through re-education training to make sure they end up woke. We can see why parents opposing this type of consulting would be bad, right?

But, to be fair to Garland, who has been heralded as an accomplished federal judge and a fair-minded attorney, he at least went to the DOJ counsel and obtained an analysis of the ethics of the situation, right? My understanding is that any federal employee, which would include Garland, can ask for an ethics opinion on a potential conflict of interest. If a federal attorney clears them, at least they double-checked first.

"Are you refusing to answer if you found an ethics telling you—" Cruz said.

The *New York Post* reported:

> "There's no possible—" Garland attempted to respond."So you're saying no; just answer it directly. You know how to answer a question directly. Did you seek an ethics opinion?"
>
> "I'm telling you that if I thought there was any reasonable—if there was a conflict of interest, I would do that," Garland said."[68]

68 Callie Patteson, "AG Garland's son-in-law's education company supports critical race theory," *New York Post*, October 13, 2021, https://nypost.com/2021/10/27/cruz-spars-with-garland-over-son-in-laws-education-company/

It's not clear he did; he refused to tell Senator Ted Cruz if he obtained one, and if he did obtain one clearing the situation, why wouldn't he just say it?

CRT does not just infect our schools, however. It also infects our military. Instead of planning for the proper withdrawal from Afghanistan, our troops and military leaders were busy learning about CRT, leading to one of the greatest atrocities so far of the Biden administration: the botched, and deadly, pullout from the country.

CHAPTER 4

OUR MILITARY LEADERS LEAVE OUR TROOPS BEHIND

President Joe Biden made the correct decision to follow President Trump's plan to withdraw our troops from the long war in Afghanistan. But he utterly botched it for several reasons, one being that he had made "diversity" and CRT and other woke nonsense a priority of the DOD. The purpose of the DOD should not be to push a leftist social agenda but to protect Americans.

Let's start with General Mark Milley. The anti-Trump military leader said he thinks troops should read CRT books such as those of Boston University Professor Ibram X. Kendi. Perhaps Milley was so enthralled with *How to Be an Antiracist* that he did not have time to study a map of Afghanistan, consult with intelligence, or prepare a proper withdrawal. Thanks to that, Americans were left stranded and thirteen troops died during the failed pullout.[69]

Miranda Devine, writing for the *New York Post*, put it eloquently.

"Our 13 young military fallen deserved better, but they died with honor and give us faith in their noble generation, which has had to shoulder the burden of its feckless elders," Devine wrote. "A war that began when most of them were babies ended in disgrace when they were killed along with nearly 200 Afghans in last week's suicide attack at Kabul airport during a withdrawal that could not have been more botched."

"The chaos in Kabul is not business as usual. It is not the inevitable result of ending a 20-year-war. It is not the price you pay for evacuating refugees," she wrote. "There is nothing to boast about. Heads should be rolling. Generals should be falling on their swords. Yet all we get is smirks and sly spin from a White House consumed by optics."

The mother of fallen hero Rylee McCollum shared this sentiment. "They had months and months to remove everyone from Afghanistan and they chose not to. And so they sent in freaking 6,000 troops and my son, through the laws of statistics, my son was one of the ones who just got blown up by a freaking terrorist bomb yesterday. So instead of grieving and crying, I'm just getting mad."[70]

---

69 Miranda Devine, "13 US service members died in Afghanistan because terrible leadership let them down: Devine," *New York Post*, August 29, 2021, https://nypost.com/2021/08/29/13-us-service-members-dead-in-kabul-due-to-bad-leaders-devine/

70 Miranda Devine, "13 US service members died in Afghanistan because terrible leadership let them down: Devine," *New York Post*, August 29, 2021, https://nypost.com/2021/08/29/13-us-service-members-dead-in-kabul-due-to-bad-leaders-devine/

Where was Biden? Where was General Milley? They seemed too focused on pushing a woke agenda and trying to get the troops to take a COVID-19 vaccine. Biden, of course, initially blamed Trump.

But former military officials, those who served our country honorably, could see right through it.

"One former senior official, who spoke on condition of anonymity, said that under President Biden, top officials held meetings on 'culture war' issues every week, and sometimes more," Fox News reported in September 2021. "The roster of those attending included Secretary of Defense Lloyd Austin and the secretaries of all the military departments, that official said."[71]

Let's stop for a second. In the middle of what should have been time spent strategizing how to safely evacuate our armed forces, our civilian personnel, contractors, and billions of dollars' worth of equipment, what do you think the top military brass were discussing? In a world where we had a president who knew that his job is to be Commander-in-Chief and not a Chief Diversity Officer, the answer would be clear: the military officers and the Secretary of Defense would discuss how to secure key airports in the country and how to work with the Afghan army to protect us as we left. There'd be a concrete plan in place to ensure that the metaphorical last man there isn't in danger.

---

71 Maxim Lott, "'Woke' issues distracted leaders from Afghanistan, former military officials say," Fox News, September 28, 2021, https://www.foxnews.com/politics/afghanistan-military-officials-distracted-woke-issues

But instead, our military leaders—and I'm not talking about our brave men and women in uniform who serve admirably, sacrifice their livelihoods, and work hard every day to keep them safe but about the chairsitters like General Mark Milley—focused on the following:

"They never met once on readiness. But they met every week on transgender issues, extremism, racism, sexual assault, sexual harassment, et cetera," the military official told Fox News.

As he points out, it's one thing if there's a one-hour presentation about how to treat all troops with respect and how to increase social cohesion among our men and women in uniform. But at the end of the day, wasting time on woke nonsense takes time away from the primary purpose of the U.S. military, which is to protect our country.

"There's only 168 hours in a week. They were spending all their time on these things, particularly early on. Yes, they were distracted," an official told Fox News.

"The U.S. military was slow to adjust its withdrawal plans even as the Taliban began taking the country piece by piece throughout the summer, culminating in the fall of Kabul and the seizure of billions of dollars of U.S.-supplied military equipment," Fox News reported.

Yes, though it's painful to look back on that, particularly for anyone reading this book who served in Afghanistan, it must be noted how President Biden, General Milley, and Secretary Lloyd Austin have endangered people in the future. It's one thing if, to save American lives, we have to blow up a helicopter as we leave; life is more valuable than any object.

But when we leave the Taliban armed with the best weapons American taxpayer dollars can buy, it's as if we wiped away years of work to stabilize the region.

Ammoland.com created a list of American weapons left in Afghanistan. Now I want you to think of anti-American terrorists fully armed with these weapons to understand the magnitude of Biden's failure. This is why he is a dangerous president.

"No one has done more to strengthen the ability of the Taliban in their mission to perpetrate evil on the World than Joe Biden. While desperately trying to destroy the 2nd Amendment, Democrats are simultaneously handing over $83 billion worth of training and equipment to the enemy in a botched retreat from Afghanistan," Dan Wos wrote.[72] "Aside from the fact that the Biden Administration pulled our military out while leaving unarmed and defenseless American Citizens behind, the enormous list of weapons and true military hardware that was gift-wrapped and handed to the Taliban is of great concern," he wrote.

The list includes more than 208 pieces of aircraft, including "45 UH-60 Blackhawk Helicopters" and "30 Military Version Cessnas." Taliban terrorists can drive to those aircraft in any of the "75,989 Total Vehicles: FMTV, M35, Ford Rangers, Ford F350, Ford Vans, Toyota Pickups, Armored Security Vehicles" left there.

72 Dan Wos, "Full List of American War Weapons Lost in Afghanistan," Ammoland, December 5, 2021, https://www.ammoland.com/2021/12/full-list-of-american-weapons-left-afghanistan/

Other weaponry left behind, according to Ammoland, includes:

- 61,000 M203 Rounds
- 20,040 Grenades
- Howitzers
- Mortars +1,000's of Rounds
- 162,000 pieces of Encrypted Military Communications Gear
- 16,000+ Night Vision Goggles
- Newest Technology Night Vision Scopes
- Thermal Scopes and Thermal Mono Googles
- 10,000 2.75 inch Air to Ground Rockets
- Reconnaissance Equipment (ISR)
- Laser Aiming Units
- Explosives Ordnance C-4, Semtex, Detonators, Shaped Charges, Thermite, Incendiaries, AP/API/APIT
- 2,520 Bombs
- Administration Encrypted Cell Phones and Laptops ALL operational
- Pallets with Millions of Dollars in US Currency
- Millions of Rounds of Ammunition including but not limited to 20,150,600 rounds of 7.62mm, 9,000,000 rounds of 50.caliber

- Large Stockpile of Plate Carriers and Body Armor
- US Military HIIDE, for Handheld Interagency Identity Detection Equipment Biometrics

This is truly a disgrace.

This led to an embarrassment for the DOD and President Biden when a video and photos circulated of the Taliban holding a parade with our weapons.

Or at least it should have. But as of this writing, about six months after the botched pullout, Secretary Austin and General Milley are still in office.

Department of Defense report: Biden failed America in Afghanistan

An official report from the U.S. Army concluded that Biden failed America—a claim he quickly dismissed. Now that Trump is out of office, liberals are okay with questioning the insight of military leaders again.

The two-thousand-page report does not look good on Biden, and history should show that he failed America and our troops.

The *Washington Post* summarized the results, though it has yet to publish the full report, so who knows what other terrible things are mentioned in the document. This is, after all, Jeff Bezos' paper.

"Beyond the bleak, blunt assessments of top military commanders, the documents contain previously unreported disclosures about the violence American personnel experienced, including one exchange of gunfire that left two Taliban fighters dead after they allegedly menaced a group of U.S. Marines and Afghan civilians," the *Washington Post* reported. "In a separate incident a few days later, U.S. troops killed a member of an elite Afghan strike unit that had joined the operation and wounded six others after they fired on the Americans."[73]

"The investigation was launched in response to an Aug. 26 suicide bombing just outside the airport that killed an estimated 170 Afghan civilians and 13 U.S. service members," the *Post* reported. "But it is much broader, providing perhaps the fullest official account yet of the evacuation operation, which spanned 17 nightmarish days and has become one of the Biden administration's defining moments—drawing scrutiny from Republicans and Democrats for the haphazard nature in which the United States ended its longest war."

Navy Rear Admiral Peter Vasely said policymakers ignored information from commanders on the ground. "He did not identify any administration officials by name, but said inattention to the Taliban's determination to complete a swift and total military takeover undermined commanders' ability to ready their forces."

This is at the feet of Biden. But also at the feet of Austin and Milley, who were too busy sitting comfy in

73 Dan Lamothe and Alex Horton, "Documents reveal U.S. military's frustration with White House, diplomats over Afghanistan evacuation," *Washington Post*, February 12, 2022, https://www.washingtonpost.com/national-security/2022/02/08/afghanistan-evacuation-investigation/

D.C. drinking tea and reading about antiracism and white privilege to ensure that our brave men and women in uniform were safely evacuated from the country and that it did not immediately turn into a Third World hellhole run by Islamic theocrats. Biden's team even ignored our ambassador there; remember that this is the person on the ground who is getting information from other sources on the ground. National Security Adviser Jake Sullivan sits in the White House or Eisenhower Building and gets his news from CNN or MSNBC, not from military personnel, Afghan intelligence assets, or contractors.

"[Ambassador Ross] Wilson wanted two weeks to evacuate the embassy and leave a skeleton staff at the airport, military officials said. But by Aug. 12, three days before Kabul's fall, Secretary of State Antony Blinken and White House national security adviser Jake Sullivan called Wilson and instructed him to move more quickly, Vasely told investigators," the *Post* reported.

So, what does Biden do in the face of this report? Does he say, "I made a mistake; I am again sorry for the lives lost; I'm ordering a commission to study what else we did wrong so that in the future we can ensure our troops are not evacuated in such a poor way ever again"?

Nope. He rejected the findings. Just like that. Imagine if you received a bad performance review at work and just said "I disagree" without any self-reflection.

"No, that's not what I was told," Biden said, telling NBC News' Lester Holt that people in the administration said he wasn't to blame. Well, duh! Those people are probably also implicated in the report; they have an interest in pushing the blame back to the actual people in Afghanistan (whom they ignored). "There was no good time to get out, but if we had not gotten out, they acknowledged we would have had to put a hell of a lot more troops back in," Biden said.

"I am rejecting them," Biden said, when asked about his stance on the report.

The rejection drew condemnation from both sides of the political aisle.

Republican Senate Minority Leader Mitch McConnell criticized Biden for rejecting the findings without evidence that there were flaws in the report. "While the world's eyes are fixed on this present foreign policy crisis, troubling facts are continuing to surface surrounding the Administration's previous self-inflicted crisis—the botched retreat from Afghanistan...The report hammers home a damning fact we've known for months: The Biden Administration received clear advance warnings from commanders on the ground that should have been heeded, but went ignored. As I warned at the time, we have confirmation this disaster was foreseeable, foreseen, and avoidable," McConnell said on the Senate floor on February 16. "The Army's conclusions build upon the report from the Special Inspector General which was declassified last month. While President Biden and his political advisors still cling to the notion they got mistaken advice and were caught off-guard, both these reports suggest that non-partisan experts knew and predicted the Afghan military would likely collapse and spent months trying in vain to get the Administration to pay attention."[74]

"Top commanders reported that trying to get State Department officials to engage in advance evacuation plans was 'like pulling teeth,'...That the National Security Council was 'not seriously planning for an evacuation.'

"That, among peers in uniform, 'everyone clearly saw some of the advantage of holding Bagram,'" McConnell said, lambasting his former Senate colleague. "As the top U.S. commander on the ground during the evacuation put it, policymakers had not 'paid attention to the indicators of what was happening on the ground,'...This staggering report from our own U.S. Army should have chastened the Biden Administration. It should be an occasion for apology, reflection, and accountability."

But instead, Biden rejected it.

CNN's Jake Tapper called the response "insulting." Tapper is a liberal ideologue who works for a liberal propaganda station. Even he could not ignore Biden's blunders.

"It's difficult to overstate how insulting Biden's sweeping rejection is to so many service members and veterans," Tapper said. "Given the full content of the two-thousand pages of documents and this U.S. Army investigation which CNN has also obtained, many accounts are from troops who were on the ground at the gates near the canal

---

74 "Without Evidence, President Biden "Rejects" Army Report on Botched Afghanistan Policy: Republican Leader," The Republican Leader, February 16, 2022, https://www.republicanleader.senate.gov/newsroom/remarks/without-evidence-president-biden-rejects-army-report-on-botched-afghanistan-policy

around the airport, non-commissioned officers, junior officers, Joes, people with little political motivation to lie and heavy legal and moral obligation to tell the truth in sworn statements," Tapper pointed out.[75] "I don't doubt that President Biden cares, but I do not understand why he would not manifest that care into taking this investigation more seriously, absorbing the tragic details, contemplating the obvious failures of his administration, failures that cost lives."

A report from U.S. Senator James Risch provides more insight into the botched pullout. The Idaho Republican is the ranking member of the Foreign Relations Committee.[76]

"While there is substantial disagreement about the policy to leave Afghanistan, Americans share outrage over how the United States withdrew last August, and what that failure has done to America's standing in the world," Risch said in an accompanying news release. "My report describes how the Biden Administration's failure of duty allowed for a quick Taliban takeover of Afghanistan and a botched withdrawal that left hundreds of Americans and tens of thousands of Afghan partners behind. The United States will have to deal with the fallout of this failure for

75 Lindsay Kornick, "CNN's Jake Tapper calls Biden's rejection of Army's after-action report on Afghanistan 'insulting,'" Fox News, February 13, 2022, https://www.foxnews.com/media/cnn-jake-tapper-biden-rejection-report-afghanistan-insulting=

76 United States Senate Committee on Foreign Relations, "Left Behind: A Brief Assessment of the Biden Administration's Strategic Failures during the Afghanistan Evacuation," (Report, Washington, DC, February 2022), 1–65. https://www.foreign.senate.gov/download/02-03-22-risch-report-on-afghanistan

years to come, so it is imperative that we mitigate the strategic implications to ensure we do not repeat mistakes."[77]

"The Biden Administration did not hold a senior-level interagency meeting to discuss an evacuation or formally task the State Department (State) to contact at risk populations, including Americans, until August 14, just hours before Kabul fell," Risch reported. Furthermore (this is all from a summary of the report):

"The Biden Administration:

- Failed to do any contingency planning for worst-case scenarios.
- Ignored intelligence reports about the risk of an imminent Taliban takeover of Afghanistan.
- Disregarded dissent cables from Foreign Service Officers on the front lines.
- Abandoned Bagram Air Base based on arbitrary troop caps and political considerations, hampering the evacuations and the reinserted troops.
- Failed to take significant steps to improve the Special Immigrant Visa (SIV) program despite clear evidence that the program was flawed.

---

77 "Risch Publishes Report on Biden Administration's Strategic Failures During Afghanistan Withdrawal," United States Senate Committee on Foreign Relations, February 3, 2022, https://www.foreign.senate.gov/press/ranking/release/risch-publishes-report-on-biden-administrations-strategic-failures-during-afghanistan-withdrawal

The Biden Administration failed to protect:

- American citizens in Afghanistan—thousands of Americans and Legal Permanent Residents were left behind.
- Afghan partners—tens of thousands of SIV applicants were left behind, jeopardizing America's credibility and ability to recruit partners in the future.

The botched withdrawal damaged U.S. credibility with our allies."

Former military commanders said, even prior to this report, that top military brass should resign their positions. Former National Security Advisor Lieutenant General Keith Kellogg said that the failed pullout, including the Taliban's taking of Kabul, was an "abysmal failure."

"It's an abysmal failure at the strategic level. That's what the American people should be concerned about. It's a lack of decision making, it's a lack of really seeing what the problem is going forward, and it's a lack of seeing what is going on on the ground and what's happening here in Washington, D.C., at the leadership level," he said in August 2021, as Afghanistan began to fall.[78]

Kellogg, with decades of national security experience, said he believed the White House and DOD were just trying to ignore the failures.

---

78 Henry Rodgers, "EXCLUSIVE: 'Abysmal Failure At The Strategic Level' — Gen. Kellogg Slams Biden's Handling Of Afghanistan," *The Daily Caller*, August 24, 2021, https://dailycaller.com/2021/08/24/abysmal-failure-general-keith-kellogg-joe-biden-afghanistan-marsha-blackburn/

"What's happening right now, it's almost like they think it's going to go away and ignore it. They did it at the border, and have now done it with Afghanistan, and they're kind of saying, 'well maybe if we just keep ignoring it, talk about something else out there, it'll eventually go away.' I think Americans need to be concerned right now, we're seeing a real lack of what I call command and control decision making at the most senior levels," Kellogg told Senator Marsha Blackburn (R-TN).

Nearly ninety retired flag officers also saw the failures of Austin and Milley and demanded their resignation.

"If they did not do everything within their authority to stop the hasty withdrawal, they should resign," a letter published at the end of August 2021 said. "Conversely, if they did do everything within their ability to persuade the [president] to not hastily exit the country without ensuring the safety of our citizens and Afghans loyal to America, then they should have resigned in protest as a matter of conscience and public statement."

"A fundamental principle in the military is holding those in charge responsible and accountable for their actions or inactions. There must be accountability at all levels for this tragic and avoidable debacle," they wrote.

A retired Marine three-star general further explained what he calls "critical military theory." He warned that the military is losing focus when it comes to its primary purposes.

"**The U.S. military has two main purposes**—to deter our enemies from engaging us in warfare, and if that fails, to defeat them in combat. Deterrence is only possible if the opposing force believes it will be defeated. Respect is not good enough; fear and certainty are required," Lieutenant General Gregory Newbold wrote in *Task & Purpose*, a military website, in February 2022.[79]

"**To be true to its purpose, the U.S. military cannot be a mirror image of the society it serves**," he said. "Values that are admirable in civilian society—sensitivity, individuality, compassion, and tolerance for the less capable—are often antithetical to the traits that deter a potential enemy and win the wars that must be fought: Conformity, discipline, unity."

To make it clear to General Milley, this means that so-called "antiracism training," "diversity seminars," and deep reflections on "white privilege" are antithetical to killing terrorists and stopping attacks on our country.

"**There is only one overriding standard for military capability: lethality**. Those officeholders who dilute this core truth with civil society's often appropriate priorities (diversity, gender focus, etc.) undermine the military's chances of success in combat," Lieutenant General Newbold wrote. "Reduced chances for success mean more casualties, which makes defeat more likely. Combat is the harshest meritocracy that exists, and nothing but ruthless adherence to this principle contributes to deterrence and combat effectiveness."

79 Gregory Newbold, "A retired Marine 3-star general explains 'critical military theory,'" *Task & Purpose*, February 10, 2022, https://taskandpurpose.com/opinion/critical-military-theory/

Yet, our military continues to be attacked from within by leftist social engineers who want the greatest armed forces in the world to look like a drag show at Oberlin College. Consider that our Special Operations Command received its own diversity officer, a rabid anti-Trumper who had an embarrassing record of tweeting leftist political attacks.

"The newly hired head of diversity and inclusion at US Special Operations Command has been reassigned as the military conducts an investigation of his controversial social media posts, military spokesmen said Monday, including one that appeared to compare former President Donald Trump to Adolf Hitler," CNN reported in March 2021.[80] Two months into the Biden administration, a key priority was hiring a leftist.

What did Mr. Richard Torres-Estrada say? "Richard Torres-Estrada posted a June 20 photo comparison of former President Donald Trump holding a Bible outside a church to former Nazi Germany dictator Adolf Hitler," *Newsmax* reported.[81]

"Also, in a February post that was public until Monday, Torres-Estrada posted a Facebook meme suggesting Sen.

---

80 Oren Liebermann and Ellie Kaufman, "New head of diversity and inclusion at US Special Operations Command reassigned as military investigates social media posts," CNN, March 29, 2021, https://www.cnn.com/2021/03/29/politics/richard-torres-estrada-social-media/index.html

81 Eric Mack, "Special Ops Diversity Czar Reassigned for Divisive Posts," *Newsmax*, March 30, 2021, https://www.newsmax.com/politics/pentagon-diversity-hypocrisy-social-media/2021/03/30/id/1015722/

Ted Cruz, R-Texas, was 'MISSING' amid the Texas power outages and his ballyhooed travel to Cancun, Mexico," *Newsmax* said. There isn't anything wrong with Biden picking someone who is critical of President Trump; we'd expect that a Democratic president would pick liberal Democrats to fill many positions. But there are two problems with the Special Operations Command: (1) having a diversity office and (2) picking someone who is a committed leftist. Harkening back to the Newbold essay, the purpose of the military is to protect America, not to ensure that all soldiers have pronouns in their Twitter bios or can recite passages from *How to Be an Antiracist.*

A former Special Forces Warrant Officer and current Congressional candidate explained why the hiring is troublesome.

"The left is not hiding the fact that they are in control & have the power to cleanse the ranks of those who do not submit...He is one of the reason you see so much woke tweeting from Sr Mil leaders They are pledging their loyalty to the new order & cleansing themselves of the old," Joe Kent wrote on Twitter in 2021. "Special ops leans heavily right, that's why Biden's team put such an outspoken monitor in SOCCOM & is not having him tidy up his social media, it's a not so subtle warning. Special ops leans right but honorably serves our nation, regardless of what party POTUS is from."[82]

---

82 Kristina Wong, "Special Operations Command Hires Diversity and Inclusion Chief Who Posted Anti-Trump Memes," *Breitbart*, March 26, 2021, https://www.breitbart.com/politics/2021/03/26/special-operations-command-hires-diversity-and-inclusion-chief-who-posted-anti-trump-memes/

Jed Babbin, a former undersecretary in the DOD, had similar warnings about what Biden was doing to the military, though he said the president was carrying on a social agenda started under the Obama administration.

"There are two types of senior military leaders. One always seeks ways to maximize the lethality and readiness of the forces under his command. The other is so sunken in the political swamp that those concepts are nearly forgotten. Secretary of Defense Lloyd Austin unfortunately falls in the second category. He and President Biden are turning our military into a 'woke' force," Babbin wrote in March 2021 in the *Washington Times*.[83]

After giving examples of Biden's wokeness, Babbin concluded, "Mr. Biden's 'woke' military will focus on politics, not lethality and readiness. It will excel in virtue signaling and fail at winning battles and wars," a warning that came true just a few months later in August 2021, when the leftists in the military let the savage Taliban terrorists retake Kabul and reinstall an authoritarian Islamic rule in the country.

So, why is General Mark Milley still around? That's a great question that military and national security experts as well as average American citizens are asking.

Could it be because he has ties to China, and the Biden Democratic Party is close to China? After all, it was then-candidate Joe Biden who quickly condemned

---

83 Jed Babbin, "Biden's woke military," *Washington Times*, March 30, 2021, https://www.washingtontimes.com/news/2021/mar/30/bidens-woke-military/

President Trump as xenophobic for closing our borders to China at the beginning of the coronavirus outbreak.

General Milley commits treason

General Milley's job is specifically to ensure that America is protected from foreign attacks. But he seemed to believe that his job was to protect *China* from foreign attacks—meaning, from the United States.

That's apparently why he committed treason by back-channeling with China while Trump was still in office. General Milley said he would warn our number one adversary before we attacked them.

"I am certain, guaranteed certain, that President Trump had no intent to attack and it was my task to make sure I communicated that. And the purpose was to de-escalate," Milley told a Congressional committee in September 2021.[84]

"Did you or did you not tell him that if we were going to attack, you'd let him know?" Republican Vicky Hartzler asked him.

Milley tried to evade admitting to what was clearly a treasonous act.

"As part of the conversation, I said, Gen. Li, there's not going to be a war. There's not going to be an attack between great powers, and if it was, the tensions would

84 Mark Moore, "Milley admits he would tell Chinese general if US launched an attack," *New York Post*, September 29, 2021, https://nypost.com/2021/09/29/milley-admits-he-would-tell-china-if-us-launched-an-attack/

build up, there would be calls going back and forth from all kinds of senior officials," Milley said. "I said, hell, I'll call you. But we're not going to attack you. Trust me, we're not going to attack you. These are two great powers, and I am doing my best to transmit the president's intent, President Trump's intent to ensure the incident doesn't escalate," Milley said.

Lieutenant General Kellogg again criticized Milley. "I've never seen any chairman do that before. …None of them operate in that political lane like he did. And it's really kind of disturbing to me that he would do it," Kellogg said. "I think he's lost all his credibility."

But being close to China isn't a burden for the Biden administration; it's an asset.

Because President Biden's foreign policy goals often seem aligned not with American interests but with those of China and Ukraine.

CHAPTER 5

BIDEN IS COMPROMISED ON CHINA AND UKRAINE

President Joe Biden is compromised on China and Ukraine, and by extension, Russia.

Remember, it was former VP Joe Biden who went to bat for Chinese Communist Party (CCP) interests in February 2020, at the beginning of the COVID outbreak, labeling Trump xenophobic.

"We are in the midst of a crisis with the coronavirus. We need to lead the way with science—not Donald Trump's record of hysteria, xenophobia, and fear-mongering. He is the worst possible person to lead our country through a global health emergency," Biden tweeted.[85]

85 Joe Biden (@joebiden), "We are in the midst of a crisis with the coronavirus…." Twitter, February 1, 2020, https://twitter.com/JoeBiden/status/1223727977361338370?s=20

The tweet was a precursor to what would come, when our dangerous president would carry water for China.

Remember, too, that the foreign policy of President Biden began with an embarrassing meeting in Alaska. Instead of taking a tough line with China and demanding that it stop stealing our intellectual property or apologize for its role in creating COVID-19, the Biden administration went "woke."

Secretary of State Antony Blinken traveled to Alaska in March 2021 for a meeting with Chinese counterparts. It is common for a new president and his team to have visits and summits with important countries, but what they did there was a complete embarrassment to the United States.

Instead of sending a message that the United States would not let China beat it around, Blinken let the CCP embarrass us on our home field.

"Many people within the United States actually have little confidence in the democracy of the United States," the CCP foreign minister told the U.S. delegation at the March 2021 meeting. "We believe that it is important for the United States to change its own image and to stop advancing its own democracy in the rest of the world."[86]

"We hope that the United States will do better on human rights. China has made steady progress in human rights. And the fact is that there are many problems within

---

86 Steven Nelson, "Biden 'proud of team' after China mocks US at Alaska Summit," *New York Post*, March 19, 2021, https://nypost.com/2021/03/19/biden-proud-of-team-after-china-mocks-us-at-alaska-summit/

the United States regarding human rights, which is admitted by the US itself," the Chinese foreign minister said.

Blinken conceded to the Chinese that America was not perfect, while National Security Advisor Jake Sullivan talked about America's "secret sauce" of politics, as if being the leader of the greatest country in the world is akin to putting good flavoring on a meal.

"There's one more hallmark of our leadership here at home, and that's a constant quest to, as we say, form a more perfect union. And that quest, by definition, acknowledges our imperfections, acknowledges that we're not perfect, we make mistakes, we have reversals, we take steps back," Blinken groveled to the CCP. "But what we've done throughout our history is to confront those challenges openly, publicly, transparently, not trying to ignore them, not trying to pretend they don't exist, not trying to sweep them under a rug. And sometimes it's painful, sometimes it's ugly, but each and every time, we have come out stronger, better, more united as a country."

To translate: Yes, China, the United States is bad and racist and we have a terrible history but please give us time; we are trying our best. Pathetic.

The Biden family and China

His family, including, of course, son Hunter Biden, has had ties to China for a long time. The *New York Post* did an excellent job of creating a timeline, and I will touch on some of the highlights below.

"For at least seven years, many when his father was vice president, Hunter Biden pursued a lucrative deal to run an investment firm founded by millions of dollars from a Chinese partnership," the *New York Post* explained in December 2020.[87]

The *New York Post* notes that, back in June 2009, just a few months into the Obama-Biden administration, "Hunter Biden co-founded Rosemont Seneca Partners, an investment fund, along with Christopher Heinz—the stepson of Obama's future Secretary of State John Kerry—and Devon Archer, a former Kerry adviser."

"[In 2012], [a]s Joe Biden ran for his second term as vice president, Hunter Biden and Devon Archer made contact with Chinese financier Jonathan Li, who ran the private-equity fund Bohai Capital. The trio discussed a plan to become partners in a new operation that would invest Chinese cash in ventures outside the country. Eighty percent of the resulting company, Bohai Harvest, was controlled by Chinese state-owned interests," the *New York Post* reported.

The Bidens made it a family business, and used taxpayer resources for it. As the *Post* wrote about 2013: "When Chinese president Xi Jinping alarmed the rest of Asia with an aggressive expansion of his military claims over the East China Sea, Vice President Biden was dis-

---

87 Joh Levine and Mary Kay Linge, "Hunter Biden and China: A timeline of his business ties to the Far East," *New York Post*, March19,2020,https://nypost.com/article/hunter-biden-china-timeline-business-ties/

patched to Beijing to try to de-escalate tensions. The second son tagged along on Air Force Two. While a somber and subdued Joe Biden held a marathon five-hour meeting with Xi, Hunter got together with Jonathan Li in what handlers at the time described as a social visit. The son even arranged for a handshake between Li and his father at the hotel of the American delegation—troubling some of the vice president's advisors, according to the New Yorker. Ten days later, the Chinese business license for Bohai Harvest—the company that Hunter Biden and Devon Archer had been trying to launch for more than a year—was approved."

"[A Biden associate] emailed Hunter Biden to outline remuneration packages for Hunter and five other people in an unspecified business venture. The email—found on the Hunter Biden laptop and exposed in a bombshell report by The Post—suggested equity shares were being assigned to Biden family members, with a note indicating that 10% would be held by Hunter 'for the big guy'—who [whistleblower and investor Tony Bobulinski] later definitively identified as Joe Biden. Three days later, Bobulinski says, the plans changed: Joe Biden's 10% share would be held in the name of his brother Jim instead," the *Post* wrote.

News continues to come out about the Biden family's close ties to China. "The Biden family scored $31 million from five deals in China, all with individuals with direct ties to the Chinese spy apparatus," *Breitbart* reported in January 2022, based on information in investigative reporter Peter Schweizer's book *Red Handed.*[88] "Multiple financiers with direct ties to Chinese intelligence partnered with Hunter Biden during and after his father's time as Vice President—including the former head of the Ministry of State Security and the head of foreign intelligence recruitment—and some of those relationships remain intact," *Breitbart* reported.

"Schweizer explains that Beijing saw a financial relationship with the Bidens as an opening for 'elite capture,' which allowed Hunter Biden to secure meetings and score major deals with people in the highest levels of Chinese financial institutions and the Chinese Communist Party—and in return they would be able to leverage the Bidens' power for their interests," *Breitbart* reported.

The excellent investigative reporter calculated that just two deals alone netted Hunter Biden $25 million. He details in his book the shady and unethical ways the Biden family worked with CCP leaders for investment deals. "In sum, each deal the Bidens secured in China was via a businessman with deep ties at the highest levels of Chinese intelligence. And in each case there appears to be little discernible business or professional service that was rendered in return for the money," he wrote.

---

88 Emma-Jo Morris, "Bombshell: Biden Family Scored $31 Million From Deals With Individuals With Direct Ties To The Highest Levels of Chinese Intelligence," *Breitbart*, January 24, 2022, https://www.breitbart.com/politics/2022/01/24/bombshell-biden-family-scored-31-million-from-deals-with-individuals-with-direct-ties-to-the-highest-levels-of-chinese-intelligence/

Let's be incredibly generous for a minute and pretend that Joe Biden has completely washed his hands of any involvement with Chinese investment deals. And that Hunter Biden truly now is just an artist who is trying to get clean.

That would not change that Biden's nominees and personnel have questionable ties to China.

President Biden's President and Chair of the Export-Import (Ex-Im) Bank, Reta Jo Lewis, has eyebrow-raising ties to the Chinese. Remember that the Ex-Im Bank is responsible for providing financial support to American companies that want to sell overseas, meaning that it has great power to subsidize the sale of goods to allies, or adversaries.

Fox News reported on the nomination in December 2021, before Lewis' confirmation.[89]

"The EX-IM Bank represents crony capitalism at its worst, providing taxpayer-financed giveaways to large corporations and foreign governments like China," Senator Pat Toomey warned. "The bank has a history of forcing American taxpayers to support loans to the Export-Import Bank of China and even the Bank of China itself," the Republican moderate said. "I am not convinced Ms. Lewis will end these subsidies to the Chinese government,

89 Caitlin McFall, "Biden's Export-Import Bank nominee's strong pro-China ties cast doubt on her confirmation," Fox News, December 8, 2021, https://www.foxnews.com/politics/bidens-export-import-bank-nominee-pro-china-ties-confirmation

which is just one of many reasons why I am opposing Ms. Lewis' nomination."

"Lewis' current position as a 'strategic adviser' for the United States Heartland China Association (USHCA)—a bipartisan group dedicated to fostering relations between the U.S. and China—has raised GOP eyebrows," Fox News reported. "At a time of increasing competition with China, it is also troubling that President Biden has nominated someone who seems more interested in coordination with China than competing with them," Republican Senator Cynthia Lummis's office told Fox News.

Senator Marco Rubio said that the Biden administration needs to be tougher on China. "We are now at a period of time where the issue with China is so critical, we can't afford to send or put into positions of great influence anyone who isn't clear about the threat China poses and how strong we have to be about it. We've already waited too long to address this," the Florida Republican said.

Lael Brainard, a Biden nominee to be Vice Chair of the Federal Reserve, has her own troubling ties to China.

"Lael Brainard, Biden's pick for Vice Chairman at the Federal Reserve, worked against both political parties to alleviate pressure on China for their currency manipulation while working for the Obama administration," the website BidenNoms.com explains. "Around that time, both Republican and Democrats expressed concern over China undervaluing its currency, which manipulates the markets, and went so far as to draft legislation to protect the market from China's behavior, but she ignored those concerns and concluded that China is not a currency manipulator."[90]

While working in the Treasury Department under the Obama administration, Brainard helped play down China's currency manipulation, which directly harms American consumers.

She oversaw reports that concluded that China did not manipulate currency, even though the evidence is overwhelming that the CCP does.

Just a few years later, Trump's Treasury Secretary Steve Mnuchin would conclude that, while the communist country's actions did not meet technical requirements under a specific law for manipulating currency, other actions taken by the CCP clearly meet the definition of it.

"Based on the analysis in this Report, Treasury determines, pursuant to [a trade law], that China continues to warrant placement on the Monitoring List of economies that merit close attention to their currency practices," a 2019 report said.[91] "Treasury determines that while China does not meet the standards identified in Section 3004 of the 1988 Act at this time, Treasury will carefully monitor

---

90 "Despite Bipartisan Action Against China's Currency Manipulation, Lael Brainard Does the Opposite," Bidennoms, January 3, 2022, https://www.bidennoms.com/news/1350/bipartisan-action-against-chinas-currency-manipulation-lael-brainard-does-the-opposite

91 U.S. Department of the Treasury, "Macroeconomic and Foreign Exchange Policies of Major Trading Partners of the United States" (Report, Washington, DC, 2019), https://home.treasury.gov/system/files/206/2019-05-28-May-2019-FX-Report.pdf

and review this determination over the following 6-month period in light of the exceptionally large and growing bilateral trade imbalance between China and the United States and China's history of facilitating an undervalued currency. Treasury continues to have significant concerns about China's currency practices," the 2019 report said.

In layman's terms: China continues to cheat.

"Brainard is a nominee that chooses to ignore positive bipartisan efforts to hold China accountable for their malicious economic behavior and should be rejected for any leadership position at the Fed," the American Accountability Foundation, which runs the Biden nomination tracking website, concluded in its January assessment of the nominee.

Bidens and Ukraine

As this book is written, President Biden seems ready to lead us into the war in Ukraine. What is our interest in Ukraine? It's not clear. But why might Biden and the Democrats be so keen on taking us into war there? Lee Smith with the *Epoch Times* has an excellent analysis we will look at now before returning to a reminder on Hunter Biden's dealings in the country.

"For all the theories the media and Beltway experts have advanced to explain the perhaps imminent Eastern European conflict, they've hidden one big piece of the puzzle—the political faction that Biden leads sees Ukraine as an instrument to advance its narrow partisan interests, foreign and domestic," Lee Smith wrote on January 27, 2022.[92]

"In 2013, the Obama administration saw a Ukrainian protest movement as an opportunity to topple a Kyiv government aligned with Moscow. A few short years later, Hillary Clinton's presidential campaign used Ukrainian officials and activists to push an intelligence operation targeting her rival, Donald Trump," Smith noted. He pointed out that U.S. policymakers worked with the Ukrainian government to destabilize the United States through sham impeachment proceedings against Trump.

But before the Trump administration, the Obama team was trying to handpick a new leader for Ukraine. "As violence erupted in the Ukrainian capital [in 2013], senior Obama administration officials seized the opportunity to remold the government to their own liking. Assistant Secretary of State Victoria Nuland and U.S. Ambassador to Ukraine Geoffrey Pyatt were famously caught on tape discussing the prime minister they were planning to install. The tape was allegedly leaked by the Russians to show how the United States was interfering in the internal political dynamics of a foreign country," Smith wrote.

"Ukrainian American activist Alexandra Chalupa, sought help from the Ukrainian embassy in smearing Trump as a Russian agent. The Ukrainian ambassador to

---

92 Lee Smith, "What's Behind the Troop Buildup on the Ukraine—Russia Border," *The Epoch Times*, February 1, 2022, https://www.theepochtimes.com/whats-behind-the-troop-build-up-on-the-ukraine-russia-border_4237796.html

Washington pitched in with an anti-Trump op-ed in *The Hill*," in 2016, Smith notes. Russia hoax purveyor Fusion GPS was also getting intelligence from Serhiy Leshchenko, a Ukrainian parliamentarian. There's also, of course, Ukrainian Alex Vindman's role in the sham impeachment.

Smith concludes that the Democratic Party has been using Ukraine for ten years now, so Biden is fine sending our brave men and women to fight a war against Russia. "America is now governed by corrupt officials who squandered their prestige and forfeited the national interest for the purpose of undermining their own political system. Because Ukraine was their instrument, a Biden administration is dangerous to Russia on Russia's border."

The White House has already sent $2 billion to Ukraine, and Congress and Biden are itching to send more.[93]

No wonder Biden wants to use American troops to fight wars in Russia. President Biden has frequently failed to articulate a clear and forceful agenda for Ukraine. He seems itching to take us to war there but has failed to take basic steps that could have prevented the invasion into Ukraine. He failed to put strong sanctions on Putin and Russia before the invasion, sanctions that could have deterred the war and saved thousands of lives.

93 "Fact Sheet on U.S. Security Assistance for the Ukraine," The White House, March 16, 2022, https://www.whitehouse.gov/briefing-room/statements-releases/2022/03/16/fact-sheet-on-u-s-security-assistance-for-ukraine/#:~:text=President%20Biden%20today%20announced%20an,start%20of%20the%20Biden%20Administration.

Foreign policy expert Gordon Chang explains how Biden botched the Ukraine situation in comments to both Fox News and *The Epoch Times*.

"What you say to Putin is, 'I'll take the sanctions off if you withdraw your forces from the Ukraine border. If you stop threatening another country.' But Biden didn't do that," Chang told *Epoch TV*. "I think we are heading to a global conflict, because Biden is not willing to exercise American power…and right now I think we are probably at a point where we are too late to stop general conflict around the world," Chang said in February 2022.[94] He shared similar sentiments with Laura Ingraham at Fox News. "China has made it very clear that they are financing the war against Ukraine. And the United States warned China not to do this on February 3," Chang said.

But, Chang warned, the "elites" do not want to interfere with their investments in China. Meanwhile, thousands of Ukrainians suffer. President Biden also primed the war in Ukraine by failing on American energy, allowing Putin to dominate the energy markets.

The money from the five hundred thousand barrels of oil a day the United States bought from Russia helped fund the war in Ukraine. There's no doubt that Putin invaded Ukraine because he knew President Biden

94 Matt Lamb, "Russian invasion could lead to World War III, China expert tells Epoch Times," LifeSiteNews, March 4, 2022, https://www.lifesitenews.com/news/russian-invasion-could-lead-to-world-war-iii-foreign-policy-expert-warns/

would not respond correctly. That's why he took over the Crimea under Obama but did not invade any place while President Trump was in office. Putin respected (or feared) Trump's swift action and strong leadership.

Senator Joe Manchin, a West Virginia Democrat, has repeatedly called out Biden for undermining American national security through his left-wing Green New Deal policies.[95] "The entire world is watching as Vladimir Putin uses energy as a weapon in an attempt to extort and coerce our European allies," Manchin said in February 2022. "While Americans decry what is happening in Ukraine, the United States continues to allow the import of more than half a million barrels per day of crude oil and other petroleum products from Russia during this time of war."

He said further:

This makes no sense at all and represents a clear and present danger to our nation's energy security. The United States can and must ramp up domestic energy production and increase access to our abundant resources and technologies to both protect our energy independence and support our allies around the globe.

If there was ever a time to be energy independent, it is now. I am calling on the Administration and industry partners to take action immediately, up to and including banning crude oil imports from Russia. To continue to

---

95 "Manchin Rings Alarm On Continued Russian Crude Oil Imports," US Senate Committee on Energy and Natural Resources, February 28, 2022, https://www.energy.senate.gov/2022/2/manchin-rings-alarm-on-continued-russian-crude-oil-imports

ask other countries to do what we can do for ourselves in a cleaner way is hypocritical. To continue to rely on Russian energy as they attack Ukraine is senseless. Manchin is half-right: Biden would have been right to ban Russian oil *and* ramp up American energy independence. But as of this writing, Biden has only banned the importation of Russian oil and done little to increase oil production. Maybe Hunter Biden could help us get some Ukrainian natural gas.

Hunter and Ukraine

The son of a liberal Democrat who opposes American natural gas and oil received a sweet consulting detail worth millions of dollars for a Ukrainian natural gas company despite not speaking the language. Sounds suspicious, huh?

Let's take a bit of a dive into the Hunter Biden-Burisma deal in case you forgot or never knew the extent of how bad it was.

At the time, VP Joe Biden had been tasked by President Obama with rooting out corruption, which the current president used as a pretense to fire a prosecutor looking into Burisma.

The *New York Post* has an excellent summary with new information that it reported on in February 2022; let's start there.

"A classified US State Department email from 2016 shows a leading diplomat warning that Hunter Biden's lucrative job with a Ukrainian energy company 'undercut' American efforts to fight corruption in the Eastern European country," the *New York Post* reported.[96] "In the Nov. 22, 2016, email, former State Department official George Kent, then the deputy chief of mission at the US Embassy in Ukraine, recounted a discussion in which he detailed the 'saga' surrounding the graft case against Mykola Zlochevsky, a former Ukrainian natural resources minister and founder of Burisma Holdings, which paid Hunter Biden $1 million a year to sit on its board."

"From May 2014, Burisma Holdings Ltd. was paying Hunter $83,333 a month to sit on its board, invoices on his abandoned laptop show," the *Post* previously reported. But as soon as daddy left the vice presidency, Hunter's pay went down. Why? Generally, the longer you stay at a company the more you make, and it seems rare for board members, brought in to provide expertise and guidance, to make less money. Could it be because Hunter was no longer as valuable because he couldn't call up dad and ask him to push Burisma-friendly policies?

"After [March 2017], the amount listed on Hunter's monthly Burisma invoices was reduced to $41,500, effective from May 2017. The amount was paid in Euros, at the rate of between 35,000 Euros and 36,100 Euros per month, based on currency fluctuations at the time," the *New York Post* reported. Still not a bad deal.

What were his job duties?

---

96 Bruce Golding, "Classified 2016 email shows US diplomat warning of Hunter Biden deals in Ukraine," *New York Post*, February 2, 2022, https://nypost.com/2022/02/02/us-diplomat-warned-about-hunter-biden-ukraine-deals-in-2016/

"During his time on the board of one of Ukraine's largest natural gas companies, Hunter Biden, the son of former U.S. Vice-President Joe Biden, was regarded as a helpful non-executive director with a powerful name, according to people familiar with Biden's role at the company," Reuters reported in October 2019.[97]

"Interviews with more than a dozen people, including executives and former prosecutors in Ukraine, paint a picture of a director who provided advice on legal issues, corporate finance and strategy during a five-year term on the board, which ended in April of this year," Reuters reported. "[Hunter] never visited Ukraine for company business during that time, according to three of the people." Democrats downplayed the whole issue. But an official U.S. Senate report came to a different conclusion. To be fair, it's from a Republican-led committee, but let's look at some of the facts and see what conclusion we might come to.[98]

---

97 Polina Ivanova, Maria Tsvetkova, Ilya Zhegulev and Luke Baker, "What Hunter Biden did on the board of Ukrainian energy company Burisma," Reuters, October 18, 2019, https://www.reuters.com/article/us-hunter-biden-ukraine-idUSKBN1WX1P7

98 U.S Senate Committee on Homeland Security and Governmental Affairs, "Hunter Biden, Burisma, and Corruption: The Impact on U.S. Government Policy and Related Concerns" (Report, Washington, DC), 1–87, https://www.hsgac.senate.gov/imo/media/doc/Ukraine%20Report_FINAL.pdf

Ukrainian foreign policy—guided by the Biden family bank account?

"In late 2013 and into 2014, mass protests erupted in Kyiv, Ukraine, demanding integration into western economies and an end to systemic corruption that had plagued the country. At least 82 people were killed during the protests, which culminated on Feb. 21 when Ukrainian President Viktor Yanukovych abdicated by fleeing the country. Less than two months later, over the span of only 28 days, significant events involving the Bidens unfolded," the 2020 U.S. Senate report concluded.

"On April 16, 2014, Vice President Biden met with his son's business partner, Devon Archer, at the White House. Five days later, Vice President Biden visited Ukraine, and he soon after was described in the press as the 'public face of the administration's handling of Ukraine.'" Hey, that's curious!

"The day after his visit, on April 22, Archer joined the board of Burisma. Six days later, on April 28, British officials seized $23 million from the London bank accounts of Burisma's owner, Mykola Zlochevsky. Fourteen days later, on May 12, Hunter Biden joined the board of Burisma, and over the course of the next several years, Hunter Biden and Devon Archer were paid millions of dollars from a corrupt Ukrainian oligarch for their participation on the board," the report said.

"What the Chairmen discovered during the course of this investigation is that the Obama administration knew

that Hunter Biden's position on Burisma's board was problematic and did interfere in the efficient execution of policy with respect to Ukraine," the report continued. "Moreover, this investigation has illustrated the extent to which officials within the Obama administration ignored the glaring warning signs when the vice president's son joined the board of a company owned by a corrupt Ukrainian oligarch. And, as will be discussed in later sections, Hunter Biden was not the only Biden who cashed in on Joe Biden's vice presidency."

The report is eighty-seven pages long and is titled "Hunter Biden, Burisma, and Corruption: The Impact on U.S. Government Policy and Related Concerns," in case you'd like to go look it up and read the whole thing. Feel free to make your own judgment. But here are some of the highlights that, in my opinion, show that there are very questionable ties among Hunter, President Biden, and the family at-large.[99]

Note: Mykola Zlochevsky, mentioned below, is the founder of Burisma.

- "In October 2015, senior State Department official Amos Hochstein raised concerns with Vice President Biden, as well as with Hunter Biden, that Hunter Biden's position on Burisma's board enabled Russian disinformation efforts and risked undermining U.S. policy in Ukraine."

99 Ibid.

- "Former Assistant Secretary of State for European and Eurasian Affairs Victoria Nuland testified that confronting oligarchs would send an anticorruption message in Ukraine. [George] Kent told the Committees that [Mykola] Zlochevsky was an 'odious oligarch.' However, in December 2015, instead of following U.S. objectives of confronting oligarchs, Vice President Biden's staff advised him to avoid commenting on Zlochevsky and recommended he say, 'I'm not going to get into naming names or accusing individuals.'"
- "In addition to the over $4 million paid by Burisma for Hunter Biden's and [Devon] Archer's board memberships, Hunter Biden, his family, and Archer received millions of dollars from foreign nationals with questionable backgrounds."
- "Archer received $142,300 from Kenges Rakishev of Kazakhstan, purportedly for a car, the same day Vice President Joe Biden appeared with Ukrainian Prime Minister [Arseniy] Yasenyuk and addressed Ukrainian legislators in Kyiv regarding Russia's actions in Crimea."
- "Hunter Biden received a $3.5 million wire transfer from Elena Baturina, the wife of the former mayor of Moscow."

Patriotic, hard-working Americans who run small businesses and put in sixty- to seventy-hour weeks are derided by socialists like Elizabeth Warren and AOC and Bernie Sanders as greedy fat cats. But when the son of a senator, VP, and now president makes millions primarily trading on his name, many leftists are suddenly very quiet. In liberal D.C. "logic," if you make money providing a good or service that people want, such as cars, homes, or computers, you're greedy. But if you fly to China or Ukraine and sit in on a couple of meetings while helping transact millions of dollars all with a wink and nod about your dad's position of influence, it's all fine with Chucky Schumer and Nancy Pelosi.

"As the Chairmen's report details, Hunter Biden's role on Burisma's board negatively impacted the efforts of dedicated career-service individuals who were fighting to push for anticorruption measures in Ukraine," the report concluded. "Because the vice president's son had a direct link to a corrupt company and its owner, State Department officials were required to maintain situational awareness of Hunter Biden's association with Burisma."

"Unfortunately, U.S. officials had no other choice but to endure the 'awkward[ness]' of continuing to push an anticorruption agenda in Ukraine while the vice president's son sat on the board of a Ukrainian company with a corrupt owner. As George Kent testified, he 'would have advised any American not to get on the board of Zlochevsky's company.'" Yet, even though Hunter Biden's position on Burisma's board cast a shadow over the work of those advancing anticorruption reforms in Ukraine, the Committees are only aware of two individuals who raised concerns to their superiors. Despite the efforts of these individuals, their concerns appear to have fallen on deaf ears."

Put in other words, the State Department had to be very careful about how they dealt with international corruption lest they cross paths with one of Hunter Biden's questionable business practices.

Could the same problem happen at a local art show?

Biden the painter—but who buys his art?

Before going further, I want to make something clear: The issue with Hunter Biden's dealings is that they are a national security risk and they are rife with the potential for corruption. All it takes is one Ukrainian investor who learns more dirt about Hunter and suddenly the United States is shaping our foreign policy not on the interests of what will keep all Americans safe but on what will keep Joe's son out of prison.

Everyone knows by now that Hunter has struggled with drug abuse. If he chooses to take up painting and art as a healthy habit and as part of a recovery program, that is great for him. But he continues to engage in questionable business practices.

Even CNN found Biden's art dealings questionable.

"Hunter Biden is facing renewed questions about whether his art career could pose a conflict of interest for his father's work in the Oval Office after recent images

from a glitzy private showing shot across social media," CNN reported in October 2021. "Last weekend, images posted on social media and shared in the press emerged showing Hunter Biden displaying his work in Los Angeles at Milk Studios—a Hollywood venue that typically hosts video and photo shoots."[100]

Why is it an issue that Hunter is at his own art show? Because there are serious concerns that international buyers could use him as a conduit to buy influence in the White House. Let's imagine two scenarios where this could happen, one that would be a classic D.C. swamp tactic and another that would be both corrupt AND be a serious national security problem.

Scenario one: The CEO of a solar company that needs the White House to help it import solar panels from China buys paint from Hunter and, bada bing bada boom, word gets back to Dad Biden. Suddenly, the solar company's shipments are able to get through customs without any issue and Hunter gets $500,000. Classic D.C. swamp tactic of giving money to the relative or a friend of someone in power to get noticed and buy goodwill.

Scenario two: One of the many Chinese or Ukrainian cretins needs to get something from Biden, so they send $1 million to Hunter for his artwork. Suddenly, foreign oligarchs and Hunter's bank account are the main

---

100 Maegan Vazquez, "Hunter Biden's private LA art show renews conflict-of-interest concerns," CNN, October 9, 2021, https://www.cnn.com/2021/10/09/politics/hunter-biden-los-angeles-art-show/index.html

motivators of our foreign policy. We know this has happened before—that's what the Senate report on Burisma concluded!

The White House had previously said that Hunter would not be at the art show and would not know who bought his art. A government accountability expert criticized Hunter's presence.

Danielle Brian of the Project on Government Oversight said Hunter's attendance "undermined the White House's early claims that neither he, nor the White House, would know who bought his art."

"The silver lining to this dark cloud is now the rest of us also know the universe of who might be interested in buying the paintings—which will make it easier to track if those people are attempting to curry favor with the White House through the President's son," Brian told CNN.

"No one in our family and extended family is going to be involved in any government undertaking or foreign policy," Joe Biden promised. Democrats spent four years complaining that President Trump appointed family members such as Ivanka Trump and her husband Jared Kushner to governmental roles. But here's the difference—his kids' work was out in the open and it was made clear what projects and policies they were carrying out. If Biden wants to appoint one of his kids to an actual government position that is subject to public records laws and accountability that's one thing—the issue is when Hunter is just always hanging around, gobbling up money from foreign entities and it takes congressional hearings to find out the connection between Hunter's business and his dad's policies.

An art expert said Hunter's work is not even good. "How much of that value is due to the art itself? That's easy: None of it," Maryland art professor Jeffry Cudlin told the *Washington Examiner* when asked about Biden's work that was getting sold for up to $500,000.[101]

"Though Biden's artwork might raise an eyebrow or two, none of his paintings were particularly memorable, Cudlin said. They might fetch between $850-$3,000 for a buyer 'to hang over someone's couch,'" the *Washington Examiner* reported. "If Hunter Biden were applying to school to get a BFA in painting, I think a portfolio with these pieces in it would indicate some sense of the medium, some nascent talent, and encourage anyone reviewing it that with a little training and a little study, Biden might one day make some interesting paintings," Cudlin told the conservative publication.

So where does this get us?

It can be fun to mock Hunter's artwork, but what is the real issue here? The Biden family hides behind a folksy, down-to-earth image while raking in millions from shady foreign entities. Meanwhile, our southern border is being

---

101 Charles Hilu, "Is Hunter Biden's art worth $500,000? Here's what a curator has to say," *Washington Examiner*, July 4, 2021, https://www.washingtonexaminer.com/news/hunter-biden-what-art-curator-says

attacked daily by illegal migrants. Maybe if Hunter had investments in Mexico or Texas it would get Joe's attention.

President Biden is not just dangerous because of his own, leftist agenda but also because of who surrounds him. He has put together a cabinet of liberal ideologues, political insiders, and altogether incompetent picks. He has picked someone to oversee our healthcare system who is a committed supporter of late-term abortions and used the Attorney General's office in California to sue Catholic nuns who provide nursing home care to poor, elderly people. He picked someone to be his VP who led the charge on leveling falsehoods against Brett Kavanaugh and who climbed her way up in politics by having adulterous relationships with the speaker of the house in California, getting well-paid government appointments despite having little experience. He picked someone to be his Transportation Secretary who could not even keep the potholes filled as mayor. We're only a year and a half into the Biden presidency, so there's still plenty of time for him to continue to pick awful, incompetent, and dangerous nominees. Let's take a look at some of them. Since this book already covered the radical politics of AG Merrick Garland, the anti-parent stance of Education Secretary Miguel Cardona, and the woke, CRT obsessiveness of Defense Secretary Lloyd Austin, this portion will cover those in other positions.

Pete Buttigieg—The Democratic wunderkind who failed to manage transportation policy in his own city.

Transportation Secretary Pete Buttigieg's crowning achievement and why he is so well-liked in the Democratic Party appears to be solely that he is a homosexual in a homosexual "marriage" with a man. As mayor of South Bend, Indiana, he had a very simple job when it came to transportation policy: keep the potholes filled and the roads paved and ensure that pedestrians are able to safely walk around the city. He failed at that and now oversees billions of dollars in transportation funding and also sets the federal policy for the Department of Transportation.

Ironically, for Buttigieg's support for abortion through all nine months of pregnancy and his support for homosexual "marriage," it took a company founded by a conservative Catholic to fix the pothole problem in his city.

"Many residents feel the city has the worst pothole situation in the state. So many, in fact, that they reached out to Domino's Pizza to do something about it. And Domino's agreed," the *South Bend Tribune* reported in January 2019. "On Monday, the national pizza company announced the city of South Bend will receive a $5,000 "Paving for Pizza" Grant to fill in potholes. The grant, created in 2018, asks customers to nominate their hometown to repair potholes so carryout pizza can have a smooth delivery ride home. Domino" consumer public relations specialist Danielle Bulger said only one grant is given per state. South Bend was named Indiana's recipient."[102]

One year earlier, the hometown paper ran a story that said the situation with potholes was the worst in at least 15 years. "This is number one or two in my memory," a mechanic told the *South Bend Tribune*. "The other real bad year was back 12 to 15 years ago."[103]

Insurance agents and tow truck companies also agreed that the pothole situation was awful.

It's not just the potholes that he failed on—he failed on basic sidewalk and crosswalk safety—and when a young black kid was killed, he seemed to blame the child for it.

In January 2017, a young black boy and his brother were walking in South Bend when, suddenly, the young boy was fatally struck by a car. The street had been made into a two-way street as part of Buttigieg's "Smart Streets" project. What did the man who is now tasked with overseeing highways, ports, and airports say?

"We simply don't know whether it would have made any difference yesterday morning as two children darted across the street, at an angle, and one of them, outside the

---

102 Mary Shown, "South Bend receives $5,000 grant from Domino's Pizza to fill potholes," *South Bend Tribune*, January 7, 2019, https://www.southbendtribune.com/story/business/2019/01/07/south-bend-receives-5000-grant-from-dominos-pizza-to-fill-potholes/46357453/

103 Ed Semmler, "Potholes around South Bend might be worst in recent memory," *South Bend Tribune*, February 26, 2018, https://www.southbendtribune.com/story/news/local/2018/02/26/potholes-around-south-bend-might-be-worst-in-recent-memory/46492695/

crosswalk, was struck and killed," Buttigieg said.[104] Yep. He blamed the kid.

But now he's going to tackle racist roads? The Transportation Secretary has said his department will tackle racist roads.

"There is racism physically built into some of our highways, and that's why the jobs plan has specifically committed to reconnect some of the communities that were divided by these dollars," Buttigieg told *The Grio*.[105] Here's the truth—yes, some cities did build highways in such a way to divide neighborhoods—fifty to seventy years ago. There is no racism *imbued* in the concrete and asphalt. And big cities have primarily been run by liberal Democrats for decades now—will more spending fix an old problem? Now more people have cars and there is more public transit—the physical divisions are disappearing.

But Mayor Pete, as his fans used to call him, should have started in South Bend if he wanted to stop discriminatory practices. A radio host in Indiana explained that Mayor Pete's "Smart Streets" project harmed black people the most beyond the young black boy killed partially due to Pete's policy.

---

104 Jeff Parrott, "South Bend mayor stands behind Smart Streets after traffic death," *South Bend Tribune*, January 25, 2017, https://www.southbendtribune.com/story/news/local/2017/01/25/south-bend-mayor-stands-behind-smart-streets-after-traffic-death/116976776/

105 April Ryan, "Buttigieg says racism built into US infrastructure was a 'conscious choice,'" *The Grio*, April 6, 2021, https://thegrio.com/2021/04/06/pete-buttigieg-racism-us-infrastructure/

"[Buttigieg] has zero success in infrastructure planning in South Bend at all," South Bend-based radio host Casey Hendrickson said. "Everything he touched that dealt with transportation was a miserable failure, including smart streets, which got Tristan [Moore] killed—and he was warned about that. He was told that there [are] serious issues," the radio host told Tucker Carlson in February 2022.[106] The "Smart Streets" project made it harder for first responders to get to certain areas. "And there are some high-crime areas around there that would primarily affect minorities in South Bend," Hendrickson said. "And he's actually made it a lot worse for them to get aid from first responders than before."

Did Buttigieg do this deliberately? Probably not—he probably did not intend to harm minorities, which would make it a racist policy, putting into place plans that treat one race worse than others. But the former McKinsey consultant could be fairly accused of pursuing a liberal, academic idea over common sense with deadly results.

He would bring a record of pursuing bad policies, or remaining inactive, while others suffered, to the Department of Transportation. Just six months into his time in office, Secretary Buttigieg took eight weeks off work, while our ports were clogged and the supply chain suffered, for paternity leave. Now, basic biology tells you that, because Buttigieg is a (1) man in a relationship with a (2) man, he would not need eight weeks to recover from

106 Hannah Grossman, "Radio host blasts Pete Buttigieg for 'zero success' improving infrastructure as mayor," Fox News, February 18, 2022, https://www.foxnews.com/media/radio-host-pete-buttigieg

giving birth. Neither would his "husband," Chasten. But without much fanfare (warning) he took off for eight weeks in the middle of the summer for paternity leave. Now, fathers spending time with their kids is great—but there are plenty of jobs he could have taken that would allow him to have generous paternity leave and not shirk on his duties while millions suffered due to the shipping backlog in our ports. He even posed for a dumb photo in the hospital with his two adopted kids and his "husband"—leading many on social media to wonder why he was in a hospital bed.

He also has shown to be out of touch with the average American. His mindset is that of a former McKinsey consultant, not of the hard-working plumber or truck driver who needs gasoline to go to work every day to help keep America running. In the middle of the ongoing surge in gas prices, an issue that should be the focus of the Transportation Secretary, Buttigieg suggested a simple solution—just buy an electric car!

"Clean transportation can bring significant cost savings for the American people, as well," he said on March 7, 2022. "Last month, we announced a $5 billion investment to build out a nationwide electric vehicle charging network, so that people from rural to suburban to urban communities can all benefit from the gas savings of driving an EV."[107]

---

107 Grant Atkinson, "Buttigieg: Buy a $56,000 Electric Car, So You Don't Have to Worry About Gas Prices Anymore," Western Journal, March 8, 2022, https://www.westernjournal.com/buttigieg-buy-55000-electric-car-dont-worry-gas-prices-anymore/

Never mind that there are not charging stations across the country as of today. Never mind that electric batteries are of questionable reliability and safety (an electric battery in a car reportedly caused a cargo ship to catch fire in the Atlantic Ocean).[108] Most Americans do not have $40,000 or $50,000 to spend on an electric car at the drop of a hat. Most Americans, who are struggling under the Biden economy to buy groceries, are not going to be able to suddenly go out and get a new car.

When judging someone's actions, we should, of course, take the most charitable approach. So, let's say that Buttigieg really just does not understand that most Americans cannot afford an electric car and the infrastructure of charging stations is not there yet. And let's assume that he truly believes that electric batteries are safe and reliable.

Doesn't that make him all the more dangerous? The man who does not know what he doesn't know is dangerous. In all the pie charts and spreadsheets Buttigieg has looked at, how does he not understand the importance of American oil to the economy? Of course, Buttigieg also displays an out-of-touch mentality because the price of oil does not just affect gas prices—it affects the prices of thousands of goods.

One great trait of President Trump, a trait that Biden's team needs to adapt, is acknowledging what he does not

108 Andrew J. Hawkins, "EV batteries could complicate recovery of burning cargo ship with thousands of cars," The Verge, February 18, 2022, https://www.theverge.com/2022/2/18/22940790/cargo-ship-fire-vw-porsche-lamborghini-ev-battery

know. Trump is known to ask a lot of questions of his advisors and consultants and then make a decision. That's what made him a great president—while the media will try to portray him as arrogant, he actually was very good, based on reports, on asking questions to learn more. That is what made him a great president.

But being out of touch and having a poor track record in previous jobs makes Buttigieg a perfect fit for the Biden administration—just ask DOE Secretary Jennifer Granholm.

Jennifer Granholm—Thinks it's funny that gas prices are soaring.

Secretary Granholm previously served as the governor of Michigan—trying to carry water for her, *M Live* had to say that she was dealt a "bad hand" on the economy. "And so Granholm leaves office on the morning of Jan. 1 [2011] much as her three predecessors did, leaving to her successor, Rick Snyder, a troubled state whose prospects nonetheless show signs of improvement," the paper said.[109] "Probably no one could have held off the economic tide that began to turn in 2000 as the domestic auto industry was cresting at 2 million Michigan jobs," *M Live* reported. "Net employment was to slide by 630,000 more jobs through Granholm's two terms. And Michigan's national ranking

---

109 Peter Luke, "Despite all the setbacks, Jennifer Granholm's governorship shows signs of success as it comes to a close," Michigan Live, December 19, 2020, https://www.mlive.com/politics/2010/12/despite_all_the_setbacks_jenni.html

in per-capita income dropped from 18th to 37th." Now she is in charge of Biden's job-killing energy agenda.

But even her energy agenda as governor was awful.

The conservative Mackinac Center for Public Policy highlighted some of her failures as governor.

"When U.S. Secretary of Energy Jennifer Granholm was Michigan's governor from 2003 through 2010, she championed programs granting hundreds of millions of state taxpayer dollars to so-called green energy companies," Mackinac's *Cap Con* reported in August 2021. "Granholm stated then the corporate handouts would create thousands of jobs and make Michigan the green energy capital of the world."[110]

But that did not happen. "A 2012 state auditor general report revealed that the companies receiving grants from the [green energy program] created just one-third of the jobs they promised."[111]

Some examples from the Mackinac Center will suffice:

- "Mascoma Corporation produced cellulosic ethanol and was given $20 million in state funds and an additional $100 million from the federal government, even though the firm

110 Jamie A. Hope, "Granholm Brings Michigan's Failed Green Energy Subsidies To Washington," Michigan Capital Confidential, August 7, 2021, https://www.michigancapitolconfidential.com/29009

111 Jarrett Skorup and Matthew Needham, "State Program Awards $67 Million, Creates One-Third of Projected Jobs," Michigan Capital Confidential, June 28, 2012, https://www.michigancapitolconfidential.com/17146

admitted it had experienced previous losses and had no experience in creating biogas, a substitute for natural gas or propane. The company never broke ground on a facility expected to create 70 jobs, and only three were ever reported. The state recovered $6 million of what it gave to the company."

- "Working Bugs LLC was given $2 million by the state for its green energy product. It continues to exist on a small scale but no longer produces green energy products."
- "Astraeus Wind manufactured wind turbine blades and received $6 million from the state and $7 million from the DOE. However, the company appears to no longer be operating in Michigan."
- "United Solar Ovonic made solar panels and was given $17.3 million in tax credits. It promised 700 jobs, but filed for chapter 11 bankruptcy in 2012."

Michiganders *still* aren't safe from Granholm's policies. She, Biden, and leftist current Governor Gretchen Whitmer are working hard to shut down a pipeline in the state, even as energy prices continue to skyrocket.

The Line 5 pipeline carries oil and gas from Canada into Wisconsin and Michigan. Some of that is used to heat homes during frigid Midwestern winters.

"Whitmer is unilaterally attempting to shutter the Line 5 pipeline, which transports 540,000 barrels of crude oil and natural gas liquids to refineries across the region," an opinion piece in *The Hill* said. "If successful, her actions would effectively remove the United States from the 1977 Transit Pipelines Treaty, which guarantees the uninterrupted transport of light crude and natural gas liquids between Canada and this country."[112] While the authors, Mackinac Center's Jason Hayes and Michael Van Beek, said she is doing it unilaterally, the shutdown has the support of Biden and Granholm. They certainly aren't out holding press conferences trying to stop her either.[113]

High energy prices are not a laughing matter for the family of six trying to keep gas in their van, the small business owner trying to gas a fleet of trucks, or the small town trying to ensure they can pay to keep their fire trucks and ambulances with full tanks to provide lifesaving care.

But it is to Secretary Granholm. While millions are paying more at the pump and more for groceries, Biden's Secretary of Energy laughed off a question from *Bloomberg News* about her plan to address the skyrocketing costs of energy.

"What is the Granholm plan to increase oil production in America?" Tom Keene asked her in November

---

112 Jason Hayes and Michael Van Beek, "Michigan's governor blocks more trade than the truckers did," MSN, February 2022, https://www.msn.com/en-us/news/politics/michigan-s-governor-blocks-more-trade-than-the-truckers-did/ar-AAU3RO5

113 Ibid.

2021. "That is hilarious." She then went on to blame OPEC for causing prices to rise—even though it's directly tied to the far-left, AOC-Bernie Sanders Green New Deal agenda pursued, and detailed in this book. Within days of taking office, Biden and Harris cut oil production capabilities by 40 percent, and then they seriously wonder why prices went up 40 percent or more. It's really simple supply and demand that everyone in week two of Advanced Placement Microeconomics could tell you.[114]

Secretary of Energy Granholm is a liberal ideologue who wants to pour billions and billions of dollars into "green energy" projects that will likely not materialize and will just waste taxpayer dollars. She failed as a governor—there's no reason to believe her record will be stronger as Energy Secretary.

Then again, Biden's team is chockful of people who failed in state government—just look at this VP.

VP Kamala Harris—A liberal ideologue.

One topic that VP Kamala Harris and AG Xavier Becerra might talk about is how they used government resources to harass pro-life journalists. Becerra, who succeeded Harris as the AG of California, carried on her work of filing criminal prosecutions against pro-life journalist David Daleiden.

---

114 Thomas Catenacci, "'That Is Hilarious': Energy Secretary Cackles When Asked About Rising Gasoline Prices," *The Daily Caller*, November 5, 2021, https://dailycaller.com/2021/11/05/jennifer-granholm-energy-department-gasoline-prices-opec/

Daleiden is the one who made a series of undercover videos exposing Planned Parenthood's role in the trafficking of fetal body parts. Planned Parenthood butchers babies to death and then sells their body parts, and Daleiden exposed this. As much as liberals love to talk about the free press and would get all angry if Trump called CNN "fake news," the second-highest person in the White House sicced law enforcement on a journalist.

"I hope that all Americans...are going to be able to come together to oppose the kind of radical disrespect and contempt for the First Amendment and for First Amendment civil liberties that Kamala Harris has demonstrated throughout her career," Daleiden told Sean Hannity in August 2020. "As California's attorney general, Harris sued Daleiden through an [unprecedented] application of an eavesdropping law, which he alleges was intended to [suppress his work]," Fox News reported in August 2020. "In 2015, Daleiden released secretly recorded videos of Planned Parenthood officials discussing fetal tissue procurement. The videos sparked a media firestorm and prompted federal scrutiny that continues five years after their release."[115]

It included a *raid* on Daleiden's home. "Under Harris, California authorities raided Daleiden's home for evidence—prompting questions about her relationship with

115 Sam Dorman, "Pro-life journalist David Daleiden rips Kamala Harris' 'radical disrespect and contempt' for First Amendment," Fox News, August 12, 2020, https://www.foxnews.com/politics/david-daleiden-kamala-harris-contempt-first-amendment

Planned Parenthood, which has donated to her and many other Democrats."

As Senator, Harris did the bidding of Planned Parenthood and the abortion industry by smearing Brett Kavanaugh as a rapist, even though to this day there is no proof that Christine Blasey Ford was assaulted by the now-Supreme Court Justice.

But Harris' political career is one of questionable tactics. While she believes in using state power to convict pro-life journalists, she famously urged supporters to donate to a bail fund to let violent rioters and looters out of prison—a bail fund that later helped an alleged domestic violence suspect out of prison. That man has been charged with murder after leaving prison.[116]

She had an adulterous affair with Willie Brown, the speaker of the California state assembly and later mayor. In a column, he admitted he helped boost her political career, getting her two well-paid political appointments.[117] He also helped connect her to donors.

Brown appointed his adulterous girlfriend Harris to the "California Medical Assistance Commission" and the "Unemployment Insurance Appeals Board." She received

---

116 Joshua Rhett Miller, "Bail fund backed by Kamala Harris freed Minneapolis man charged with murder," *New York Post*, September 8, 2021, https://nypost.com/2021/09/08/bail-fund-backed-by-kamala-harris-freed-man-charged-with-murder/

117 Willie Brown, "Willie Brown: Sure, I dated Kamala Harris. So what?," *San Francisco Chronicle*, January 25, 2019, https://www.sfchronicle.com/opinion/article/Sure-I-dated-Kamala-Harris-So-what-13562972.php

around $400,000 in total for serving several years between the two boards.[118]

She did not pick up any staff management skills there, or as a district attorney, AG, or U.S. Senator. Reporters have found that Harris's staff is in disarray and there is conflict between her and Biden.

VP Harris might be a good person in other aspects of her life, but as the VP, she is not up for the job.

Her office is repeatedly losing staff members—while high turnover can be normal in D.C., someone working for Harris is already in one of the most prestigious positions, working for the president and VP. It's not the same as a scheduler or entry-level constituent services staffer leaving a freshman congressman's office to work on a prestigious committee like the Senate Judiciary.

Harris lost two top communications professionals after less than a year in the White House. "[Chief spokesperson Symone] Sanders is the highest profile exit and the second high-profile one from the Harris team in the last month. Ashley Etienne, Harris's communications director, is also set to depart in the coming weeks," Politico reported in December 2021.[119] Commenting on the Sanders role in

118 Dan Morain, "2 More Brown Associates Get Well-Paid Posts: Government: The Speaker appoints his frequent companion and a longtime friend to state boards as his hold on his own powerful position wanes," *LA Times*, November 29, 1994, https://www.latimes.com/archives/la-xpm-1994-11-29-mn-2787-story.html

119 Eugene Daniels, Christopher Cadelago and Daniel Lippman, "Symone Sanders to leave the VP's office," Politico, December 1, 2021, https://www.politico.com/news/2021/12/01/symone-sanders-vice-president-office-523660

transitioning Harris and Biden into the White House, Politico said it has been difficult.

"It wasn't always smooth. Harris' office has been beset by disorder, bad press, and, at times, internal frictions. Outside advisers complained that she was handed policy issues that were destined for failure and not given what she needed to succeed as vice president."

Staff disarray, friction, poor management—it's a common theme inside the Harris office. Now, to be fair, every political staffer comes with his or her own agenda, priorities, and styles. That's common in the White House, but also common in every small or large organization. But it's reflected in the poor leadership record of VP Harris, who has not been the shining star I think many Democrats hoped she would be. It's fair to speculate that Democrats wanted Harris to be the face of the administration and be prepared to step in as president if Biden died or resigned in office—his name recognition and likeability among a swath of the population that still viewed him as a regular guy fighting for blue-collar America would get the team into the White House, and then leftist Harris could pursue a far-left agenda (which they have, but it has not been sold well or considered a good idea by most Americans).

Even the liberal *Atlantic* could not ignore the issue of Harris's managerial problems.

"Harris has been an elected official for 18 years straight, but she has only a few senior aides on staff who have worked for her for more than a few months," *The Atlantic* reported in a primarily fawning article about the VP. "Turf battles have been a recurring feature of Harris offices over the years, but her newest circle believes it is finally getting her on track after years of past staffers not serving her well. Some have been surprised at how much work there is to be done, whether that's briefing her on certain policy issues or helping her improve her sparring-with-journalists skills."[120]

The lack of a quality staff has led to confusion and disappointment, especially on a key area of concern for many Americans—immigration.

As thousands of illegal migrants flooded our border, seeing the writing on the wall that the new administration would likely let them stay, President Biden originally tasked VP Kamala Harris with dealing with the situation at the border.

But months and months went by, without a concrete plan, and Harris had not traveled to the border to speak with Border Patrol agents to see the damage wrought by criminal migrants who trespass on Americans' private land and trash it.

"President Joe Biden has tapped Vice President Kamala Harris to lead the White House effort to tackle the migration challenge at the U.S. southern border and work with Central American nations to address root

---

120 Edward-Isaac Dovere, "What Kamala Harris Has Learned About Being Vice President," *The Atlantic*, May 17, 2021, https://www.theatlantic.com/politics/archive/2021/05/kamala-harris-vice-president-impossible/618890/

causes of the problem," the Associated Press reported on March 24, 2021.[121]

"Harris is tasked with overseeing diplomatic efforts to deal with issues spurring migration in the Northern Triangle countries of El Salvador, Guatemala and Honduras, as well as pressing them to strengthen enforcement on their own borders, administration officials said," the AP reported at the time. "She's also tasked with developing and implementing a long-term strategy that gets at the root causes of migration from those countries."

It took less than a week for the liberal media to try to point blame at Republicans, claiming they were trying to "make her the face of the border crisis." But in a way, that's what Biden did, right? He said she would be in charge of border issues—so isn't she the face of all issues related to the border?

"Aides define her official task as leading the diplomatic outreach to Central American countries to address the root causes of migration. But Harris has already been tied to the border situation at large, as Republicans seek to conflate her more narrowly defined role with the entire border crisis," CNN reported. "While Biden has blamed the situation on former President Donald Trump and pent-up demand, the administration has not been clear publicly on who is in charge of the complete response."

---

121 Jonathan Lemire, Nomaan Merchant, Lisa Mascaro and Aamer Madhani, "Biden taps VP Harris to lead response to border challenges," *AP News*, March 24, 2021, https://apnews.com/article/kamala-harris-lead-migrant-crisis-response-joe-biden-3400f56255e000547d1ca3ce1aa6b8e9

Huh? Yes, the administration has been clear—VP Harris is in charge. "I've asked her, the VP, today—because she's the most qualified person to do it—to lead our efforts with Mexico and the Northern Triangle and the countries that help—are going to need help in stemming the movement of so many folks, stemming the migration to our southern border," President Biden said on March 24.[122]

Just a few weeks into her assignment, the *Washington Post* also ran cover for Harris, blaming Republicans for trying to make the VP the "border czar." But that's what President Biden clearly said! That her job was to work on the root causes of migrations and stop the migration to the border.

"As the vice president wades into a new role addressing the root causes of migration out of Guatemala, El Salvador and Honduras, Republicans are rushing to connect her to the surge in migrants at the border, losing few opportunities to use 'Harris' and 'border' in the same sentence, often with 'czar,'" the *Washington Post* wrote.[123]

You know that liberals are messing up when the media says that, actually, many presidents/politicians have had

---

122 "Remarks by President Biden and Vice President Harris in a Meeting on Immigration," The White House, March 24, 2021, https://www.whitehouse.gov/briefing-room/speeches-remarks/2021/03/24/remarks-by-president-biden-and-vice-president-harris-in-a-meeting-on-immigration/

123 Cleve R. Wootson, Jr. "Republicans try to crown Harris the 'border czar.' She rejects the title," *Washington Post*, April 27, 2021, https://www.washingtonpost.com/politics/harris-gop-border/2021/04/16/c3a2f63e-9e24-11eb-8005-bffc3a39f6d3_story.html

trouble with his issue. "The GOP pile-on is an effort to link Harris to a policy that has confounded presidents of both parties for decades and threatens to overshadow Biden's handling of other major issues." Not really. Trump was stymied in some efforts by activist judges, but he was able to stem the flow of illegal migrants and used deportation powers to remove people who had overstayed visas as well as to end so-called "temporary" Protected Status that could extend indefinitely.

Harris did indeed fail on the border.

Wisconsin Representative Glenn Grothman wrote this excellent summary just a few months into Harris's time in office, so the list of failures on the border has only increased.

"On March 24, 2021, President Joe Biden tasked Vice President Kamala Harris with addressing the crisis at our Southern border. Today marks the 87th day of her tenure in this position and she has yet to visit the border to speak with Customs and Border Protection (CBP) agents, Immigration and Customs Enforcement (ICE) agents, local law enforcement officials on the ground, and see firsthand the crisis that continues to spin out of control under her and President Biden's watch," Rep. Grothman wrote.[124] "From January-May of this year, CBP has encountered roughly 712,000 people trying to cross the Southern border. For perspective, there were roughly

124 Glenn Grothman, "VP Harris Has Failed Overseeing the Border Crisis," Glenn Grothman: US Representative, https://grothman.house.gov/news/email/show.aspx?ID=7TZ5K5OUYD6FFHLP6THY7IXI5U

922,000 encounters in all of 2019 and roughly 590,000 in 2018," the congressman said. "There is a humanitarian crisis at our Southern border. People are being used and abused while the drug cartels (who are also the ones who conduct human trafficking) line their pockets."

"I was also joined by 55 of my colleagues in sending a letter directly to President Biden pointing out the facts about the border crisis and demanding he remove Vice President Harris from her role overseeing the border," he told constituents. "She is obviously not taking this great responsibility seriously because she hasn't even visited the border. Her leadership on this issue has been less than ineffective, it has been non-existent."

Only after President Trump announced he would be visiting the border did Harris make a trip—draw your own conclusions!

She said more needed to be done to address the "root causes." Harris also said people should not come to the border because they would be turned away—a statement that did not really turn out to be true.

"I want to be clear to folks in the region who are thinking about making that dangerous trek to the United States-Mexico border: Do not come. Do not come," Harris said on June 7, 2021. "I believe if you come to our border, you will be turned back."[125]

125 Christina Wilkie, "Vice President Kamala Harris visits the U.S.-Mexico border as immigration crisis continues," CNBC, June 25, 2021, https://www.cnbc.com/2021/06/25/vice-president-kamala-harris-visits-the-us-mexico-border-.html

That's not what happened though. As we would later learn, the Biden administration used secret night flights to move illegal migrants around the country. The administration also would drop single, young males off in cities across the country. These people were not turned back at all!

Here is just one story from February 18, 2022. I'll list a few more lest anyone doubt me.

"President Joe Biden's Department of Homeland Security (DHS) released more than 62,500 border crossers and illegal aliens into the United States interior in January [2022], court records reveal," according to *Breitbart.*[126]

That's seven months after Harris explicitly said that border crossers would be turned back.

"The last figure disclosed by the Biden administration revealed that from January 2021 to August 2021, more than 530,000 border crossers and illegal aliens had been released into the U.S. interior—a foreign population nearly the size of Tucson, Arizona," *Breitbart* reported in February 2022. "In January, newly released U.S.-Mexico border figures show that Border Patrol agents apprehended nearly 154,000 border crossers. It is estimated that thousands more successfully crossed the border, undetected by agents."

---

126 John Binder, "Joe Biden's DHS Frees 62,500 Border Crossers into U.S. in a Single Month," *Breitbart*, February 18, 2022 https://www.breitbart.com/politics/2022/02/18/joe-bidens-dhs-frees-62500-border-crossers-into-u-s-in-a-single-month/

A month earlier, in January 2022, *Breitbart* reported that more than 80 percent of illegals released into the United States had still not been deported (no surprise there).

"The other roughly 85 percent of border crossers and illegal aliens are successfully evading deportation from the U.S. by ditching the reporting requirements. The number of border crossers and illegal aliens evading deportation could be even higher as many could skip out on their immigration court date issued to them via [Notices to Appear]," *Breitbart* reported. The Biden administration had claimed that 75 percent of illegal migrants were complying with the requirement to stay in touch with the federal government while deportation proceedings were under way.[127]

Furthermore, let's just take a look at the Biden administration's actions on the border and see if they align with the statement by VP Harris that border crossers will be turned back and sent home. Would someone serious about this drop plans to build a wall on the southern border? Would they falsely accuse law enforcement of using whips on Haitian migrants crossing into this country?

No, of course not.

Would they spend $3 million per day to *not* build a border wall? No, of course not. Yet that's exactly what Biden and his team are doing.

---

127 John Binder, "DHS: 6-in-7 Illegal Aliens Released into U.S. by Biden Are Evading Deportation," *Breitbart*, January 12, 2022, https://www.breitbart.com/politics/2022/01/12/dhs-6-in-7-illegal-aliens-released-into-u-s-by-biden-are-evading-deportation/

"On President Biden's first day in office, he issued a memorandum blocking new border wall construction, including money appropriated by Congress for that purpose as well as Department of Defense (DOD) funds the Trump administration reprogrammed (reallocated) for border wall construction," Robert Law wrote on July 7, 2021, just several weeks after Harris told migrants not to cross the border illegally. "Biden's January 20 memorandum ordered a 60-day review of the border wall construction contracts and recommendations, but over 180 days later the Department of Homeland Security (DHS) has failed to satisfy that directive."[128]

Law, an expert with the Center for Immigration Studies, cited a report by Senator James Lankford (R-OK) on the direct cost of not building the wall. This does not include the increased costs from illegal migrants.

"[Senator] James Lankford finds that between $1.837 billion and $2.087 billion of taxpayer dollars have been wasted since Biden's inauguration, and that this fiscal drain increases by at least $3 million per day," Law wrote. "Lankford notes that at the end of the Trump administration, approximately $10 billion had been transferred to two Department of Defense accounts for border wall construction and related projects, known as DOD 2802 Accounts and DOD 284 Accounts."

128 Robert Law, "Biden Spending $3 Million Per Day to Not Build Border Wall," Center for Immigration Studies, July 27, 2021, https://cis.org/Law/Biden-Spending-3-Million-Day-Not-Build-Border-Wall

If you remember, Trump correctly said he could use money from DOD accounts to build the border wall. This is an absolutely correct interpretation of his powers as Commander-in-Chief to protect us from invasions. We absolutely have a right to use DOD dollars to protect our borders.

"Based on interactions with DOD employees, the GOP learned that DOD 2802 accounts fund military construction projects and that there were seven border wall-related projects suspended by President Biden. Initially, the suspension resulted in $6 million a day in taxpayer waste, but after laying off some contractors the waste is down to $3 million a day," Law wrote. [129]

HHS Secretary Xavier Becerra—Took on... Catholic nuns?

HHS Secretary Xavier Becerra is a lawyer—he followed VP Harris as the AG of California. What did Mr. Becerra do as the AG of California that qualifies him to be HHS Secretary? He persecuted pro-life journalists and Catholic nuns.

The Little Sisters of the Poor is a holy group of Catholic nuns that provides care for elderly people in poverty. As Catholic nuns, they have a moral objection

129 James Lankford, "President Biden is Wasting Billions by Not Building the Border Wall" (Interim Minority Staff Report, Washington, DC), 1–36 https://www.lankford.senate.gov/imo/media/doc/GOBM%20Interim%20Report%20on%20Border%20Wall.pdf

to paying in any way for abortifacient birth control—the Catholic Church teaches that all forms of birth control are intrinsically evil.

But the Democratic Party is no longer the party of Al Smith or working-class Catholics—it serves Planned Parenthood and the abortion industry. It works on behalf of atheists and other proponents of driving Christianity out of the public square. So, AG Becerra had to go to work to do the bidding of the left-wing in California. So, he sued Catholic nuns to force them to be complicit in providing birth control they have a moral objection to.

While testifying during his nomination hearing, Becerra stunningly claimed he did *not* sue Catholic nuns.

"In 2017, Becerra, in his role as the attorney general of California, sued the Trump administration over these exemptions," the Catholic News Agency reported in March 2021. "Becerra's lawsuit, as well as a lawsuit by Pennsylvania against the administration, resulted in the nuns' appeal to the Supreme Court. The court in 2019 allowed them to intervene in the case to defend their rights, and ultimately ruled in their favor in July by upholding the Trump administration's religious and moral exemptions."[130]

"I have never sued any nuns. I have taken on the federal government, but I have never sued any affiliation of

130 Kevin J. Jones, "Despite denials, HHS nominee Xavier Becerra sued to take away nuns' religious freedom rights," Catholic News Agency, March 5, 2021, https://www.catholicnewsagency.com/news/246728/despite-denials-hhs-nominee-xavier-becerra-sued-to-take-away-nuns-religious-freedom-rights

nuns," Becerra claimed. But it was the rights of the nuns that were at stake.

But that's not the only time Becerra refused to protect the rights of Catholics.

"In another case involving Becerra and nuns, a group of Catholic nuns was affected by the state's universal abortion coverage mandate. They did not fight the mandate in court, but did file a complaint with the civil rights office at the Department of Health and Human Services. The Missionary Guadalupanas of the Holy Spirit alleged that their religious freedom was being violated by having to provide abortion coverage in health plans," the Catholic News Agency reported. "The HHS office in January 2020 ultimately found that Becerra violated federal conscience laws, and gave him 30 days to comply with the law. Becerra refused, and in December the agency announced it would withhold $200 million in Medicaid funds to California."

Support for abortion is part of Becerra's political DNA—and now he will use that position to push for billions more in taxpayer-funded abortions to kill more babies in the womb.

One longtime pro-life activist warned about his nomination.

"Becerra has a decades' old track record of siding with the abortion lobby whenever possible and using the power of his office to try and force others to share his enthusiastic support of abortion up until the moment of birth," Kristan Hawkins wrote in February 2021 for *USA Today.* [131]

The president of Students for Life of America pointed out that Becerra worked hard during the COVID lockdowns to ensure abortion vendors could send dangerous chemical abortion drugs to women so they could continue to kill their babies. Remember that the Food and Drug Administration, which regulates abortion drugs, is under HHS.

"Becerra filed 15 felony charges against the pro-life journalists who uncovered the fact that Planned Parenthood had a side business in selling aborted infant body parts," Hawkins wrote, in reference to the war Harris and Becerra waged against a free press. "I fear what Becerra might do to force government-run healthcare and abortion on his fellow citizens with a roomful of activist attorneys and the power of a huge federal budget at his disposal," Hawkins warned.

The pro-life Susan B. Anthony List said that Becerra has a "record of abortion extremism."[132]

It highlighted his support for late-term abortions when scientists have determined that babies can feel pain. He also is a supporter of "partial-birth abortion," which is

---

131 Kristan Hawkins, "Xavier Becerra, Biden's pick for head of HHS, is in trouble for good reason," *USA Today*, February 22, 2021, https://www.usatoday.com/story/opinion/2021/02/22/xavier-becerra-hhs-unqualified-and-divisive-litigator-column/6751357002/

132 "Xavier Becerra: A Record of Abortion Extremism," Susan B. Anthony Pro-Life America, https://www.sba-list.org/becerra

akin to infanticide. "In Congress, Becerra received 100% ratings from Planned Parenthood Action Fund, Planned Parenthood of California, and NARAL Pro-Choice America," the Susan B. Anthony List also noted.[133]

When it comes to pushing for legalized abortion through all nine months of pregnancy, paid for by taxpayers, Becerra is very competent. But even the White House might have *some* limits.

"The appointment of Xavier Becerra as secretary of health and human services has received a second opinion—and the diagnosis is not good," the *New York Post* reported in January 2022. "Biden administration officials are increasingly frustrated with Becerra over his response to the COVID-19 pandemic, especially the Omicron variant, the Washington Post reported…The paper added that discontent has grown to the point that replacing the former California attorney general as head of HHS has been openly discussed within the White House."[134]

National Review weighed in and said it's no surprise Becerra is a "disaster."[135]

---

133 "Xavier Becerra's Ratings and Endorsements on Issue: Abortion," Vote Smart, https://justfacts.votesmart.org/candidate/evaluations/26754/xavier-becerra/2

134 Callie Patteson, "White House frustrated with HHS chief Becerra over handling of COVID: report," *New York Post*, January 31, 2022,.https://nypost.com/2022/01/31/white-house-frustrated-with-xavier-becerra-over-covid-response/

135 Jim Geraghty, "Xavier Becerra Is a Disaster at HHS? Who Could Have Seen That Coming?," *National Review*, January 31, 2022, https://www.nationalreview.com/corner/xavier-becerra-is-a-disaster-at-hhs-who-could-have-seen-that-coming/

After all, in December 2020, the publication said that Becerra was an ideologue but not a health official. "In the midst of a once-in-a-century pandemic, Biden has selected as his administration's top health official a man who has no experience marshalling the forces of science," *National Review*'s editors wrote. "What California's top lawyer does have is plenty of experience marshalling the forces of the state to crush religious dissenters, pro-life pregnancy counselors, and independent journalists."[136]

After reviewing Becerra's leftist agenda (including opposing the merger of two religious hospital chains because they would not do so-called "gender reassignment surgeries"), *National Review* urged a rejection of his nomination. "Becerra has no medical background and no experience running a large, complex organization," the publication wrote. "Becerra's notoriety as a left-wing culture warrior will make it impossible for him to establish credibility with a significant and skeptical swath of the country."

Judge Ketanji Brown Jackson—A liberal radical.

While not a member of President Joe Biden's cabinet, his Supreme Court pick, Justice Ketanji Brown Jackson, is a hardcore leftist. She fulfilled President Biden's pledge to pick a black woman for the Supreme Court—but if confirmed (by the time you read this book), she would also

136 "No to Becerra," *National Review*, December 9, 2021, https://www.nationalreview.com/2020/12/no-to-becerra/

be an ally in advancing his liberal agenda. Jackson has a record of supporting illegal immigration, mask mandates, and legalized abortion, which has killed more than sixty million innocent babies in the past fifty years.

Carrie Severino, president of the conservative Judicial Crisis Network, said that Jackson is a "politician in robes," meaning that she gives the veneer of being an impartial jurist, but, really, she has been pushed by far-left groups to be placed on the Supreme Court to bolster a radical agenda.

"From the start of his administration, Joe Biden has made it clear that his top priority is paying back the liberal Arabella Advisors dark money network that spent over one billion dollars to help elect him and Senate Democrats," Severino warned. "These Arabella-advised groups seek nothing less than the appointment of politicians in robes who will rubber stamp their left-wing political agendas from the bench," Severino wrote for Fox News on February 25, 2022.[137]

Severino gives several examples of how Jackson is a radical leftist. For example, she represented terrorists at Guantanamo Bay, first as a public defender. That could be excused—if you're a public defender, you get stuck with whomever needs legal assistance. But she was so committed to the cause that she volunteered to take the case pro bono, even after she moved to private practice. She was so

---

137 Carrie Severino, "Supreme Court nominee Ketanji Brown Jackson, a politician in robes," Fox News, February 26, 2022, https://www.foxnews.com/opinion/supreme-court-nominee-ketanji-brown-jackson-biden-carrie-severino

committed to helping terrorists that she worked for free to help them!

"After her appointment to the district court in 2013, she compiled a record that reflected a hostility to both business and workers," Severino said. "She upheld an Obama administration meat labeling rule against a challenge from meat packers and a forest planning rule that was challenged by a coalition of timber, livestock, and off-highway vehicle organizations concerned about timber harvests falling and forest fires increasing. She also upheld a federal program that set explicit racial preferences in the awarding of government contracts."

Inflation is skyrocketing, gas is soaring, and our businesses are suffering under the Biden-AOC-Sanders agenda—and the president wants someone on the court who will be a reliable vote to uphold crushing regulations.

Furthermore, she placed her personal political beliefs above what the law said during President Donald Trump's time in office. The Trump administration wanted to expedite the deportation of illegal migrants—which is completely in the right of the executive branch to make the justice system move faster. The Trump administration did not create a new law—it sought to enforce the actual law on the books.[138] But lawless Jackson said no—remember that leftists want to make it very easy for immigrants to

138 Make The Road New York et al. V. Kevin Mcaleenan et al., 19-cv-2369 (US District Court for the District of Columbia, 2019), https://cases.justia.com/federal/district-courts/district-of-columbia/dcdce/1:2019cv02369/209974/40/0.pdf?ts=1569662340

come here illegally and stay without any worry of ever getting deported. Thankfully, a federal court later reversed her injunction.

"Though the D.C. Circuit Court of Appeals later reversed the ruling, Jackson issued a preliminary injunction to halt Trump's expanded expedited removal policy on the grounds that the administration violated the Administrative Procedure Act (APA) and did not sufficiently weigh the impact that the policy would have on illegal aliens," *Breitbart* reported.[139] Seriously? The Trump administration absolutely did weigh the impact on illegal aliens—the impact is that they would be sent home, instead of jumping in front of legal immigrants who went through the legal process to become a legal citizen.

"In a separate case, *Kiakombua v. Wolf*, the Trump administration sought to reduce asylum fraud among border crossers with an updated United States Citizenship and Immigration Services (USCIS) officer training known as the 'Credible Fear Lesson Plan' which required those claiming asylum to certify in initial screenings if they were eligible for asylum," *Breitbart* reported. "Ultimately, Jackson struck down the training to tighten up asylum fraud."

Really? How can a judge strike down a training program to assist someone in doing their job better? She did at times rule in favor of asylum processing plans, *Breitbart* noted though.

---

139 John Binder, "Biden's SCOTUS Nominee Helped Strike Down Trump's Border Controls," *Breitbart*, February 25, 2022, https://www.breitbart.com/politics/2022/02/25/bidens-scotus-nominee-helped-strike-down-trumps-border-controls/

But leftist groups see her, surely, as on their side. Pro-abortion groups like Planned Parenthood and NARAL believe she will be on their side in making it difficult for states to protect innocent babies from getting slaughtered through abortion. "Now more than ever, we need a Supreme Court justice who understands the impact of the court's rulings on people—particularly on reproductive and LGBTQ+ rights—and the importance of protecting individual liberties for generations to come," Planned Parenthood's President and CEO Alexis McGill Johnson said.[140]

NARAL, another radically pro-abortion organization, said Jackson will serve their interests well.

"Judge Jackson…has a demonstrated record of defending and upholding our constitutional rights and fundamental freedoms—including reproductive freedom. We are confident that she will be a voice for justice, equity, and freedom on the Court in the decades to come. We urge the Senate to swiftly confirm Judge Jackson," the group's president said after the nomination.[141]

---

140 Alexis McGill Johnson, "Planned Parenthood Statement on Nomination of Judge Ketanji Brown Jackson to the U.S. Supreme Court," Planned Parenthood, February 25, 2022 https://www.plannedparenthood.org/about-us/newsroom/press-releases/planned-parenthood-statement-on-nomination-of-judge-ketanji-brown-jackson-to-the-u-s-supreme-court

141 "NARAL Pro-Choice America Celebrates President Biden's Nomination of Judge Ketanji Brown Jackson to the U.S. Supreme Court," Pro Choice American, February 25, 2022, https://www.prochoiceamerica.org/2022/02/25/naral-pro-choice-america-celebrates-president-bidens-nomination-of-judge-ketanji-brown-jackson-to-the-u-s-supreme-court/

Liberal law professor raises concerns about Jackson

Liberal law professor Jonathan Turley raised serious concerns about Jackson before her confirmation to the Supreme Court. He noted that she has written only one opinion since being confirmed in 2021 to be a federal appellate judge—and that came out just twenty-four hours before President Biden officially nominated her. Her opinions as a district court judge can be lengthy, the George Washington University professor told Fox News—but they have regularly been overturned. "She has some opinions as a district court judge," Turley told Fox News. "They're quite lengthy opinions. She has been reversed, and the D.C. Circuit [Court of Appeals] reversed her for basically judicial overreach in a couple of cases."[142]

He said Judge Jackson is a "wink-and-a-nod nomination" and a "deliverable" to leftist activist groups and the liberal agenda. "Activist groups have pushed her nomination to the Supreme Court while opposing the consideration of fellow short-lister District Judge J. Michelle Childs," Professor Turley wrote in *The Hill.* "These groups clearly did not like Childs and her more moderate take on legal issues. Yet the interesting question is, what did they

142 Houston Keene, "Biden Supreme Court nominee Ketanji Brown Jackson could face scrutiny for overturned decisions," Fox News, February 26, 2022, https://www.foxnews.com/politics/ketanji-brown-jackson-biden-supreme-court-nominee-overturned-decisions

see in Judge Jackson that made her the preferred choice? It seems to be widely understood but barely discussed."[143]

He said activist groups have favored Jackson to replace Justice Stephen Breyer but "they have not explained clearly why."

That's why Jackson is a "wink and nod" nominee—she will be a likely vote for a liberal agenda, a "living constitution," and the type of judicial activism that the far-left wing of the Democratic Party has relied on to rewrite marriage, abortion, and gender laws for years. She will reliably vote against the Second Amendment and religious freedom. "Yet the confirmation process is designed to guarantee that we do not have wink-and-a-nod nominations where agendas are to be fulfilled but not discussed," Turley warned.

Time will tell if I am wrong, but history shows that Democratic nominees often advance a far-left agenda and trample on the Constitution in the name of equality or liberty or a living Constitution.

Biden's angry male staffers

Something must be said about the Biden team's poor selection of staffers. Consider his selection of TJ Ducklo. The public relations staffer had to leave after he was caught berating a reporter who asked about his relationship

143 Jonathan Turley, "Wink-and-a-nod nomination: Who really is Ketanji Brown Jackson?," *The Hill*, February 26, 2022, https://thehill.com/opinion/judiciary/595967-wink-and-a-nod-nomination-who-really-is-ketanji-brown-jackson

with a journalist. Ducklo is also the one who incredibly claimed that candidate Biden never opposed a travel ban from China.[144] His words to a reporter ended up getting him in trouble.

The issue began on January 20, 2021, the first day of the brand-new Biden administration. "In a phone conversation with [Politico reporter Tara] Palmeri, Ducklo threatened to 'destroy' her after she called his girlfriend and Axios reporter, Alexi McCammond, to discuss their romantic relationship for a story," *Breitbart* reported.[145] In a bit of unethical journalism, *Axios* allowed McCammond to continue to cover the administration, despite the fact she was dating a public relations staffer for the Biden team.

"Ducklo also accused Palmeri of focusing on the story because she was 'jealous' of a man in the past who wanted to [have sex with] his now-girlfriend rather than her. He also accused Palmeri of being 'jealous' of his relationship with his girlfriend," *Breitbart* reported.

Verbal abuse is not uncommon in the Biden White House—remember they were going to restore decency and respect to the office!

Dr. Eric Lander, a science adviser to Biden, had to resign after admitting to a history of abuse toward his

---

144 Ian Hanchett, "Biden Spox: Biden 'Was Not Against' China Travel Ban," *Breitbart*, September 10, 2020, https://www.breitbart.com/clips/2020/09/10/biden-spox-biden-was-not-against-china-travel-ban/

145 Charlie Spiering, "Joe Biden Deputy Press Secretary T.J. Ducklo Resigns over Scandal," *Breitbart*, February 13, 2021, https://www.breitbart.com/politics/2021/02/13/joe-biden-deputy-press-secretary-t-j-ducklo-resigns-over-scandal/

team. "I have sought to push myself and my colleagues to reach our shared goals—including at times challenging and criticizing," he wrote. "But it is clear that things I said, and the way I said them, crossed the line at times into being disrespectful and demeaning, to both men and women. That was never my intention."[146]

So, did he just say a few bad words or lash out once on a bad day toward employees? No, not according to Politico's reporting in February 2022.

Lander "bullied and demeaned his subordinates and violated the White House's workplace policy, an internal White House investigation recently concluded, according to interviews and an audio recording obtained by POLITICO."[147]

"The two-month investigation found 'credible evidence' that Lander—a Cabinet member and director of the Office of Science and Technology Policy who the White House touts as a key player in the pandemic response—was 'bullying' toward his then-general counsel, Rachel Wallace, according to a recorded January briefing

---

146 "Biden cabinet member Dr. Eric Lander submits resignation: 'I am devastated that I caused hurt to past and present colleagues by the way in which I have spoken to them,'" White House Wire, February 8, 2022, https://whitehousewire.com/2022/02/08/biden-cabinet-member-dr-eric-lander-submits-resignation-i-am-devastated-that-i-caused-hurt-to-past-and-present-colleagues-by-the-way-in-which-i-have-spoken-to-them-2/

147 Alex Thompson, "Biden's top science adviser bullied and demeaned subordinates, according to White House investigation," Politico, February 7, 2020, https://www.politico.com/news/2022/02/07/eric-lander-white-house-investigation-00006077

on the investigation's findings." The investigation also found "credible evidence of disrespectful interactions with staff by Dr. Lander and OSTP leadership."

The investigation found credible evidence of instances of multiple women having complained to other staff about negative interactions with Dr. Lander, where he spoke to them in a demeaning or abrasive way in front of other staff," Politico reported.

Yet, as noted by Politico, President Biden said he would fire anyone who disrespected colleagues. Only after media reporting and pressure, it seems, did Lander leave the office.

This is part of a pattern of poor selection and leadership on behalf of the White House. As a January 2022 piece in the *American Thinker* notes, the administration is incompetent.

"Could Biden's Cabinet be any more incompetent? Not likely. Jake Sullivan, his national security adviser, was part of the Russia hoax for starters and has been hopelessly awful at his job," Patrick McCarthy wrote. "Then there is Jennifer Granholm as his energy secretary, the failed former governor of Michigan who, when asked about our rising gas prices, could only laugh like a hyena. How about Pete Buttigieg as transportation secretary?" McCarthy wrote. "From unpopular mayor of South Bend to transportation czar? He was chosen because he is openly gay, not for any expertise on our national transportation and all that that entails—supply chain, shipping, interstate highways, etc."

The list goes on, and we still have two more years of this!

Conclusion: President Biden is not your average guy.

President Biden, his consultants, and the media have crafted this image of him as a likable guy that you'd want to drink beer with. He's a union man, a blue-collar kind of guy.

But, in reality, he is dangerous and vicious.

Throughout the campaign and during his time in office, Biden has used divisive, angry language to disparage people he disagrees with or to shame people into getting vaccinated.

He would start yelling, or whispering, raising concerns about his mental state.

Biden came into office with an economy primed to grow due to government lockdowns as well as a vaccine ready. Yet, less than a year later, he was using divisive language against people who made the personal choice not to get vaccinated. Here's what Biden, who is supposed be the president *for all people*, was saying in a sure sign that he had completely botched the COVID response.

"We're still in a pandemic of the unvaccinated," Biden said in August 2021. He had promised to defeat COVID by July 2021, remember.[148] "This is a pandemic of the unvaccinated," he said a month later.[149]

---

148 "Remarks by President Biden on Fighting the COVID-19 Pandemic," White House, August 18, 2021, https://www.whitehouse.gov/briefing-room/speeches-remarks/2021/08/18/remarks-by-president-biden-on-fighting-the-covid-19-pandemic-2/

149 "Remarks by President Biden on Fighting the COVID-19 Pandemic," White House, September 9, 2021, https://www.whitehouse.gov/briefing-room/speeches-remarks/2021/09/09/remarks-by-president-biden-on-fighting-the-covid-19-pandemic-3/

Then, he went in for an even darker press conference. Remember that, with COVID vaccines, it protects the person who got the shot from getting or having a severe case of COVID. So, if someone is worried about getting coronavirus, it doesn't really matter who else has gotten the shot—if they want to take the vaccine then they can. But as the Democratic Party began to lose control on coronavirus, as parents fought back against school mandates, the Democratic National Committee and its leader had to do what they often do and try to ostracize people.

"For unvaccinated, we are looking at a winter of severe illness and death—if you're unvaccinated—for themselves, their families, and the hospitals they'll soon overwhelm," the divider-in-chief said in December 2021.[150] Do you know of good leaders who blame their own people for the failures of the president?

Our country is under siege. We have a dangerous and divisive president who must be defeated and stopped from continuing to pursue the radical agenda of Bernie Sanders, AOC, and Karl Marx. Patriotic Americans are paying more at the pump and more at the grocery store and their bosses are telling them they must get injected with a vaccine in order to stay there because Biden mandated that government contractors force all employees to get vaccinated or

---

150 "Remarks by President Biden After Meeting with Members of the COVID-19 Response Team," White House, December 16, 2021, https://www.whitehouse.gov/briefing-room/speeches-remarks/2021/12/16/remarks-by-president-biden-after-meeting-with-members-of-the-covid-19-response-team/

shove a swab up their nose and take time every week to get tested for a virus that is deadly to fewer than one percent of people.

Meanwhile, illegal immigrants flood our border but we're told we must spend money defending the border—of Ukraine and Russia. Americans are looking to the president and they find someone who vacillates between anger and contempt for Americans who chose not to get vaccinated and at other times struggles to put together several sentences. They find a president who uses the full force of the federal government to go after grandmas from Indiana who briefly entered the Capitol grounds on January 6, 2021. Let me be clear—people who committed actual violence on January 6 should be fully prosecuted by federal prosecutors (as should Black Lives Matter and ANTIFA terrorists). People who assaulted others, broke windows, or stole government property should be punished, fairly. But should Anna Morgan-Lloyd, a forty-nine-year-old grandma from Indiana who "simply followed an elderly woman up some steps and into the Capitol unimpeded," have federal criminal charges stuck to her and be barred from owning a firearm?[151]

Meanwhile, for all the Biden-Harris team's talk about ending mass incarceration and creating a more equitable criminal justice system, the DOJ has been incredibly

151 Charles Creitz, "Indiana grandmother, first to be convicted in Capitol riot cases, avows nonviolence in Ingraham interview," Fox News, June 25, 2021, https://www.foxnews.com/media/indiana-grandmother-first-convicted-capitol-riot-ingraham

harsh on other January 6 defendants—despite them not posing a clear threat.

Take the example of Dominic Pezzola. "The 43-year-old veteran, now incarcerated in D.C. jail for 150 days, has been effectively shut out of his own defense in violation of constitutional guarantees specifically for defendants," *Just the News* reported in July 2021.[152] Despite Constitutional guarantees, Merrick Garland's radical DOJ has refused to allow Pezzola to see "voluminous text, audio and video evidence held by the prosecution." This is a basic right of the accused—to see the evidence against and for them so they can defend themselves.

Radical leftist Merrick Garland's DOJ has also kept Pezzola in his cell for almost the entire day, making it difficult for him to have private conversations with his attorneys to mount a legal defense. So, did Mr. Pezzola come to the Capitol with an AR-15 and one thousand rounds of ammo? Did he try to blow up a federal building? No, not even according to the DOJ's own indictment.[153]

Pezzola and others gathered in D.C. near or on the Capitol grounds. There's nothing illegal about that. Pezzola was part of a group that tried to remove barricades

---

152 Greg Piper, "January 6 inmates endure 'human rights violations on a daily basis,' bail motion alleges," *Just the News,* July 13, 2021, https://justthenews.com/government/local/dc-jail-functionally-bans-attorney-client-privilege-january-6-defendants-lawyers

153 United States v. Dominic Pezzola, William Pepe (United States District Court for the District of Columbia, 2021), https://www.justice.gov/opa/page/file/1362646/download

and assaulted cops—but the DOJ indictment does not say Pezzola hit anyone or encouraged any of that violence!

His primary counts are based on stealing a riot shield from law enforcement and then using that to break a window. ANTIFA and Black Lives Matter have burned down federal court buildings. Should Pezzola be criminally charged? Of course. But does he deserve to be kept in inhumane conditions? No.

Congresswoman Marjorie Taylor Greene has tried to get justice for the January 6 defendants. She said the conditions they are kept in are inhumane.

"While it's catch-and-release for domestic terrorists in antifa and BLM, the people who breached the Capitol on January 6 are being abused. Some even being held for 23-hours-a-day in solitary confinement," Greene said in May 2021.[154] "When will the witch hunt of Donald J. Trump and all of those who support him come to an end?" she asked.

She questioned the value behind the Nancy Pelosi-Liz Cheney January 6 commission and asked when there'd be investigations into the violent riots from Black Lives Matter and ANTIFA. "What about all the riots that happened during the summer of 2020 after the death of George Floyd? What about all the damage caused to fed-

154 Benjamin Fearnow, "Marjorie Taylor Greene Says Trump Supporters Who Breached Capitol 'Being Abused' in Fed Custody," *Newsweek*, May 18, 2021, https://www.newsweek.com/marjorie-taylor-greene-says-trump-supporters-who-breached-capitol-being-abused-fed-custody-1592629

eral buildings, churches, people's businesses and innocent people that were killed, like David Dorn?" Greene said in opposition. She brought up a black cop, David Dorn, killed during the violent Black Lives Matter riots in 2020.

Violence and actual criminal activity are often ignored by the Biden administration, which has remained largely quiet as violence has exploded, thanks to George Soros-backed prosecutors across the country.

The leftist has tried to create anarchy in America by putting into office far-left radicals who let violent criminals walk free to commit crime after crime after crime.

Soros prosecutors let criminals walk free

The Biden administration has taken a much more lenient approach to crime in the cities than the Trump White House did. It could be because the Democratic Party's donors want laxer criminal enforcement. Or the Biden-Harris team is worried about backlash from young leftist voters if they crack down on violent crime.

For all the Biden talk about inflation, he has not done anything to address another cause of inflation—stolen goods and criminal activity, which drive up costs. Of course, businesses also have to increase prices to pay for more insurance and security costs and to cover the potential for theft. Most crimes such as theft are handled by state and local authorities, but President Biden and his team can do much more to send a strong message that crime will not be tolerated. And if AG Merrick Garland can direct law enforcement to go after innocent parents who are voicing their opinions, then surely he can ask them to go after actual criminals.

Consider that George Gascon, a far-left prosecutor, has failed to stop theft from railroads in California. Biden ally and French dining enthusiast Gavin Newsom appeared to blame the train companies for constant theft. In Chicago, left-wing Mayor Lori Lightfoot, who rejected Trump's offer of help, now sees her city continue to devolve into anarchy as retail theft continues to assault the once great Chicago.

"Left-wing billionaire and Democrat donor George Soros has turned his attention in recent years to local races for prosecutor, using his money to elect 'progressives' who push 'criminal justice reform' and support the Black Lives Matter movement," *Breitbart* reported in January 2022. "The rise of these Soros-backed prosecutors has coincided with a massive surge in murder and crime in many Democrat-run cities, including many where these prosecutors have implemented radical policies toward policing and incarceration."[155]

New York City has been the victim of another Soros prosecutor.

"Newly-installed Manhattan District Attorney Alvin Bragg instructed staff on Monday that his office will not seek pre-trial detention or prison sentences for crimes

155 Joel B. Pollak, "The Soros Dozen: Big City Prosecutors Backed by George Soros," *Breitbart*, January 20, 2022, https://www.breitbart.com/crime/2022/01/20/the-soros-dozen-big-city-prosecutors-backed-by-george-soros/

other than homicide, public corruption, and a few other exceptional cases," *Breitbart* reported in January 2022.[156]

The results have been predictable. Even CNN could not ignore the issue.

"Major crimes in New York City spiked nearly 60% in February compared to the same month in 2021—a large majority occurring in a small swath of the metropolis—as Mayor Eric Adams rolled out his plan to combat gun violence and crime in the city," CNN reported in March 2022, just two months after Bragg took office. "The New York Police Department tracked increases across every major crime category. The city recorded a 41% increase in overall major crime through the first months of 2022 compared to the same period last year, including a nearly 54% increase in robberies, a 56% increase in grand larceny incidents and a 22% increase in rape reports, the data shows."[157]

Chicago's violent crime is no better. Yet, President Biden has not directed federal prosecutors there to work to crack down on potential criminal violations by looters and robbers. Merrick Garland has yet to ask prosecutors to closely watch robbers in the same way he targeted par-

---

156 Joel B. Pollak, "Soros-linked Manhattan DA Alvin Bragg: No Incarceration Except for Homicide and a Few Other Cases," *Breitbart*, January 4, 2022, https://www.breitbart.com/crime/2022/01/04/soros-linked-manhattan-da-alvin-bragg-no-incarceration-except-for-homicide-and-a-few-other-cases/

157 Emma Tucker and Mark Morales, "New York City crime wave continues into 2022 as city rolls out safety plan," CNN, March 5, 2022, https://www.cnn.com/2022/03/05/us/new-york-city-crime-wave-2022/index.html

ents. "The two-year spike in killings in Chicago mirrors a national phenomenon. At least 12 American cities saw record numbers of homicides last year, and from 2019 to 2020, the number of murders nationwide jumped 30%, the largest single-year increase in 50 years," the *Chicago Sun-Times* reported. (It's a bit of a linguistic trick to say that it's a "national phenomenon" as if every city and town is experiencing this. Leftist big cities are seeing this, which drives an overall increase. Your average town and county with normal prosecutors and leaders do not see this problem.)

"In Chicago, the increase in murders from 2019 to 2020 was 55%, according to CPD homicide data, though last year's 3% increase over 2020 trailed the national increase of nearly 7%," the newspaper reported.[158]

President Biden and the DOJ could begin by asking federal law enforcement to assist local cops in stopping crime. The DOJ also has broad power to crack down on retail theft because many of these goods that are stolen will be sold online, thus making it an interstate commerce issue. Perhaps he can ask that Montana prosecutor who seemed so keen to throw parents in jail to instead take

---

158 Andy Grimm and Tom Schuba, "Chicago's most violent neighborhoods were more dangerous than ever in 2021," *Chicago Sun-Times*, January 3, 2022, https://chicago.suntimes.com/crime/2022/1/3/22858995/chicago-violence-dangerous-murders-per-capita-2021-2020-surge-garfield-park-police-lori-lightfoot#:~:text=In%20Chicago%2C%20the%20increase%20in,first%2Dterm%20Mayor%20Lori%20Lightfoot.

more time to focus on researching how to stop theft, arson, murders, and rapes.

Biden could call together the mayors of the largest cities, almost all of whom are Democrats, and ask them to jointly work with county prosecutors to quickly bring theft, robbery, and assault charges against criminals.

Senator Chuck Grassley (R-Iowa) has demanded that the Biden administration do more to stop this out-of-control crime spree.

Senator Grassley wrote:[159]

> Organized retail crime appears to be on the rise. According to the National Retail Federation, 69 percent of retailers said they have seen an increase in organized retail crime over the last year, and 78 percent of retailers believe that greater federal law-enforcement activity would effectively combat organized retail crime. And various retail thefts have attracted the public's attention over the last few months. In November, what appears to be a flash mob of thieves ransacked at least 10 stores in San Francisco's Union Square neighborhood. The very next day, approximately 80 people attacked a Nordstrom department store in the suburban Bay Area, making off with up to $200,000 worth of merchandise in what local police called

159 Charles E. Grassley to Merrick B. Garland, December 21, 2021, https://www.grassley.senate.gov/imo/media/doc/grassley_to_justice_dept.organizedretailtheft.pdf

> "clearly a planned event." Around the same time, similar mobs attacked retail locations in the Los Angeles area stealing around $380,000 worth of merchandise, which police believe are planned attacks designed to acquire merchandise for the purpose of reselling it.

The pressure may be working, and Republicans need to keep hammering Biden on it. Just a month after Grassley's letter, Oklahoma's AG and a federal prosecutor announced criminal charges for retail theft and online sales.[160]

The situation in Chicago and New York City is in many ways an analogy for the Biden presidency. Once prosperous and safe cities have been turned into economic catastrophes where anarchy rules. Hard-working, law-abiding citizens who just want to go to work each day and provide for their families find themselves scared to go outside as violent criminals are let out on a warning and a request to come back later for a trial.

In the same way, the Biden administration has focused its efforts on pursuing parents who want to know why their kids are being taught to hate their classmates who are of a different race. An oil worker wants to know why he has been laid off from his job while the Biden administration supports the *Venezuelan* energy economy.

---

160 "Members of Retail Theft Organization Face Federal and State Charges," United States Attorney's Office: Northern District of Oklahoma, January 13, 2022, https://www.justice.gov/usao-ndok/pr/members-retail-theft-organization-face-federal-and-state-charges

A police officer who tracks down an alleged robber or murderer wants to know why he sees that same person on the news a few weeks later for *another* murder.

Even many moderates and independents, who thought Biden was a nice guy who thought about the working American, want to know why he has increasingly used discriminatory and nasty language toward their neighbor that decided not to get a COVID vaccine for personal, medical, or religious reasons.

They're wondering why the Biden administration has seemed so focused on coercing people to get the vaccine and urging mass firings of those who make a personal decision. Why are millions of immigrants allowed to flood our country while the economy is in the toilet after trillions of dollars were printed and pumped into the economy.

Young couples who were misled by the media into thinking that Trump was corrupt and that Biden would restore normalcy and a sense of order are now scratching their heads and rethinking their decision. They see Biden's son Hunter making untold amounts of money selling motel art and wonder if maybe MSNBC and CNN lied to them. They are trying to budget month to month and save for a home but they find that gas and groceries have gone up, while their salaries have not increased.

Americans want a return to safety and a booming economy

The past two years of the Biden-Harris presidency have not been good. President Biden has used demonizing rhetoric that divides Americans. He has told Americans that, if their neighbors show up to a school board meeting to ask about curriculum or protest against forced masking, those people are or are like domestic terrorists. He has told Americans to be concerned about their neighbors who have chosen not to take a COVID vaccine and to blame them if they find their local hospital is understaffed (and never mind that that hospital might have just fired people who are not getting jabbed due to an internal policy or a state order).[161]

Where do we go from here and how do we stop this most dangerous president?

First, we must speak out against President Biden. We must organize and attend rallies to protest him. We must write letters to our local newspaper and educate our neighbors about why Biden's policies are harmful.

Second, we must work to defeat the radical Democrats in Congress who are supportive of Biden's policies in the 2022 election. We must send a strong message that Americans *want* energy independence, Americans *want*

161 Matt Lamb, "New York emergency room shuts down due to lack of vaccinated nurses," LifeSiteNews, November 24, 2021, https://www.lifesitenews.com/news/new-york-emergency-room-shuts-down-due-to-lack-of-vaccinated-nurses/

secure borders, and Americans *want* the right to freedom of speech.

They *do not want* to pay nine dollars a gallon at the pump. They *do not want* to have thousands and thousands of unvetted Afghan refugees flown into the country and illegal immigrants sent around the United States. They *do not want* their friends labeled as domestic terrorists for simply speaking out at a local school board meeting.

Third, we must be relentless in going to constituent town halls or peacefully confronting our elected officials about their support for President Biden's policies. Ask your local state senator to write a letter to the White House in support of energy projects in the state. Ask your U.S. Senator or Congressman to demand answers about whether illegal immigrants are being placed into your town without anyone's knowledge.

We have many popular media sites that want to know what you are doing to fight back against the Biden administration. Reach out to the *The Daily Wire*, *Breitbart*, and *Newsmax* and let them know about how you are trying to hold your elected officials responsible and get them to speak up against Biden's far-left agenda.

We must do all work peacefully. We must fight for America's values. We must defeat the Biden-Harris-AOC agenda and put roadblocks in front of America's most dangerous president.